MEIGLE'S WW1 DEAD

The Fallen of the First World War as Commemorated on the Village War Memorial

by

Rae Taylor

Produced in association with the Meigle & District History Society

Balmacron Publishing

First published 2015 by

Published by Balmacron Publishing
Balmacron Cottage East, Meigle, Perthshire, PH12 8TD
e-mail: balmacron@virginmedia.com

ISBN 978-0-9932637-0-5

Table of Contents

Preface

Meigle's War Memorial stands between my own house and the centre of the village so I pass the memorial almost every day. When I first moved to the village my attention was immediately taken by a name from the Second World War followed by the letters "V.C." I looked into this and discovered the remarkable story of Lieutenant Commander David Wanklyn VC DSO 2 bars. Lt. Commander Wanklyn was the captain of the submarine HMS Upholder, which caused havoc to the Axis shipping in the Mediterranean from its base in Malta. Wanklyn still hold the record for the greatest tonnage of shipping sunk by any submariner in history.

My attention then moved to the list of those who perished in WW1 – which led directly to this publication. This quickly became something of an obsession, partly through the challenge of overcoming the dead ends, false leads and apparent contradictions arising from the research but also from the fascinating personal stories that I began to reveal. I hope that you will also be as interested in their stories which I have summarised.

I also sincerely hope that I have done justice to the bravery and sacrifice of these men and that this will help to keep their life stories alive in our collective memory despite their untimely deaths a century ago.

Acknowledgements

Many people and organisations have helped me in my in research, too many to mention them all individually. However, I wish to give the following particular mention:

- The staff of Perth Library, especially Dr Nicola Cowmeadow, Colin Proudfoot and Stewart Coupar, who have been superbly supportive
- The staff of the Black Watch Museum, including Richard McKenzie and Emma Halford-Forbes, who have also gone "that extra mile" to help
- DC Thompson for their permission to use the newspaper articles and photographs from the time, which were central to piecing together the stories of these men
- Tom Paton, nephew of Sergeant Thomas Brown MM, for information relating to his uncle
- Steve Baxter, great (x2) nephew of Private Frederick Baxter, for information relating to his great (x2) uncle
- Irene Wilkie, great-niece of Private Charles Gardyne Sturrock, for information relating to her great uncle
- My good friends (big) Donald Clerk, Liz Gordon and Lynda McGuigan for their advice, help and encouragement.

Despite my best efforts and all the assistance I have been given, I am sure that errors will remain, for which I take full responsibility. I have tried to comprehensively reference the source material I have used and wherever appropriate I have tried to trace, contact and obtain the permission of copyright holders. However, if anyone feels that I have inadvertently omitted or erroneously attributed such references or that I have infringed their copyright I cordially invite them to contact me.

Meigle War Memorial

Meigle War Memorial[1]

The Meigle War Memorial is located at the entrance to Victory Park on Ardler Road in Meigle. It was designed by the Dundee architectural practice of John Bruce and Sons (later Bruce, Son & Morton) and was built in 1921. It consists of a round headed arch of hammer-dressed stone[2] under a tiled "bonnet" or "reverse-gambrel" roof. This is a roof with the pitch divided into a steep slope above a shallower slope.[3] The arch is bordered on each side by recessed, curved stone bench seats. On each side of the gateway entrance to the arch is a marble memorial panel.

The plans for a War Memorial in Meigle were developed by a Committee, chaired by George Tasker of Arnbog Farm. The Memorial was unveiled on 1st October 1921 by the Duke of Atholl.[4] The Duke of Atholl was to become the driving force behind the establishment of the Scottish National War Memorial in Edinburgh which was completed in 1927.[5]

The Unveiling of Meigle War Memorial on 1st October 1921[6]

At the time of the unveiling, the left hand memorial panel was inscribed "In grateful memory of those who gave their lives for King and country in the Great War 1914-1918" whilst the other bore the names of sixteen men who gave their lives during the First World War (including their rank and regiment).[7] Today, the left hand panel contains these names, headed with the words "IN GRATEFUL MEMORY 1914-18". The right hand panel is now headed "IN GRATEFUL MEMORY 1939-45", and this is followed by the names of those who lost their lives in the Second World War.

The Panel on the Meigle War Memorial Commemorating
the Sixteen Men who Lost Their Lives in the First World War[8]

It is not entirely clear what criteria were used by the Meigle Committee for names to be included on the memorial, either in terms of the boundaries of the area defined as "Meigle" or to the nature of the links to the area which were required. This situation is not unusual as there was little consistency in the criteria used by the various war memorial committees across the country.[9]

The speeches given at the unveiling of the memorial stated that it was "to the memory of those men of that parish who gave up their lives that we might all live in security".[10] At that time, Meigle village and its parish church was at the extreme west of the area contained within boundaries of the Parish of Meigle, the Parish being quite narrow north to south but extending some distance to Eassie in the east. However, there are a number of names on the Meigle Memorial who have clear links to the village, but not necessarily to locations specifically within these Parish boundaries.

3

Taking a more inclusive definition of Meigle, all, bar one, of the sixteen men commemorated appear to have clear family links with the village. In contrast, there are others, who also lost their lives and had strong links with the village, whose names do not appear on the Memorial. Indeed, they often appear to have stronger links than many of those whose names are inscribed. However, the passage of time may prevent these anomalies from ever being properly explained.

References

[1] Photograph by the Author, taken 13 August 2006.

[2] Gifford, John, *The Buildings of Scotland - Perth & Kinross*, Yale University Press, 2007, p522.

[3] Wikipedia website, *List of Roof Shapes*, http://en.wikipedia.org/wiki/List_of_roof_shapes, Accessed 11 December 2014.

[4] Blairgowrie Advertiser, *Meigle War Memorial Unveiled*, 8 October 1921.

[5] Scottish National War Memorial website, *History*, http://www.snwm.org/content/about-history, Accessed 14 December 2014.

[6] Wilkie Irene, Personal collection.

[7] Op cit Blairgowrie Advertiser, 8 October 1921.

[8] Photograph by the Author, taken 9 November 2013.

[9] Baker, Chris, The Long Long Trail website - Great War Forum, *Criteria for putting names on memorials*, http://1914-1918.invisionzone.com/forums/index.php?showtopic=93562, Accessed 20 January 2015.

[10] Op cit Blairgowrie Advertiser, 8 October 1921.

Private Peter Younger

Peter Younger of the 6th Battalion, Black Watch was the earliest death during the First World War of those commemorated on the Meigle War Memorial but, because his surname falls towards the end of the alphabet, it is the final name on the list.

Peter Younger was born on 7th June 1866 in Dundee, the illegitimate son of Agnes Younger, a house servant.[1] As a teenager, he worked at Burnhead Farm at Auchterhouse where he lived in the adjacent cottages[2] and it was here that he met his future wife, Rachel Alcorn.

Burnhead Farm Cottages, Auchterhouse[3]

Peter and Rachel were married at the Auchterhouse Toll on 21st September 1888[4] and then the couple moved to Alyth.[5]

Peter was the head gardener on the Balhary Estate for twenty five years[6,7] where they lived in Balhary Cottar House.[8,9]

Balhary House[10]

Around 1910, they moved to Meigle, living initially at Bank Cottage when he was a janitor with the local School Board,[11,12] then later at Balmacron House.[13] Peter and Rachel had 12 children,[14] of whom all but one lived into adulthood and many to good ages.[15]

Balmacron House (Old Balmacron)[16]

Peter was in the National Reserve and was called up for service in mid March 1915,[17] joining the 2nd Supernumerary Corps of the 6th Black Watch[18] at the perhaps surprisingly old age of about 48. He was noted as being a crack shot and was a founding member of the Meigle Rifle Club.[19,20] Unfortunately, his military career was to be very short as, after being stationed in Perth for only one week, he became seriously ill and died in Woodbrae Hospital, Dunkeld just two weeks later.[21] He died on the morning of 7th April 1915 of "cardiac degeneration and dilation"[22] and was later buried in Alyth Cemetery with military honours.[23,24]

Woodbrae, Dunkeld[25]

Peter Younger's Gravestone in Alyth Cemetery[26]

Peter Younger left a widow and a family of three daughters and eight sons,[27] two of whom were serving with the Scots Guards at the time of his death.[28] Two more were also later to enlist. His eldest son, William, fought with the 2nd Battalion, Scots Guards at Loos and it was reported in April 1916 that he had "escaped without a scratch".[29] William's brother, George, was not so fortunate. George was wounded in October 1915 and invalided home, although he later recovered sufficiently to return to the front.[30]

Private William Younger, 2ⁿᵈ Battalion, Scots Guards
Peter Younger's Eldest Son³¹

References

[1] Birth registration, *Peter Younger*, Statutory Births 282/01 00992,1866 births in the 1ˢᵗ District of the Burgh of Dundee in the County of Forfar, p331.

[2] 1881 census, 3 April 1881, *Auchterhouse; ED: 2; Page: 9; Line: 15; Roll: cssct1881_77.*

[3] Photograph by the Author, taken 13 August 2006.

[4] Marriage registration, *1888 marriages in the Parish of Auchterhouse in the County of Forfar*, p3, via family tree posted on ancestry.co.uk by "golfmadbill", Accessed 14 April 2014.

[5] County of Perth Valuation Rolls, 1885-1988. CC1, No. 8 (1), 1A-213, via family tree posted on ancestry.co.uk by bucket7357.

[6] Alyth Guardian, *"A Meigle Warrior"*, 21 April 1916.

[7] Obituary, People's Journal (Perth & Perthshire), 10 April 1915.

[8] 1891 census, 5 April 1891, Parish: Alyth; ED: 6; Page: 5; Line: 18; Roll: CSSCT1891_106.

[9] 1901 census, 31 March 1901, Parish: *Alyth*; ED: *6*; Page: *6*; Line: *6*; Roll: *CSSCT1901_115.*

[10] Photograph by the Author, taken 9 August 2008.

[11] 1911 census, 2 April 1911, Census 1911 379/00 002/00 007.

[12] Op cit Obituary, People's Journal (Perth & Perthshire).

[13] Leslie's Directory for Perth and Perthshire 1910/11, 1911/12.

[14] Op cit 1911 census.

[15] Family tree posted on ancestry.co.uk by "bucket7357", Accessed 14 April 2014.

[16] Photograph by the Author, taken 7 October 2014.

[17] Op cit Obituary, People's Journal (Perth & Perthshire).

[18] Death registration, *1915 deaths in the District of Dunkeld in the County of Perth*, p3.
[19] Op cit Alyth Guardian, *"A Meigle Warrior"*.
[20] Blairgowrie Advertiser, *MEIGLE RESERVIST'S DEATH, 10 April 1915*.
[21] Op cit Obituary, People's Journal (Perth & Perthshire).
[22] Death registration, *1915 deaths in the District of Dunkeld in the County of Perth*, p3.
[23] Op cit Funeral Report, Dundee Courier.
[24] Interment Report, Perthshire Advertiser, 10 April 2016.
[25] Photograph by the Author, taken 12 December 2014.
[26] Photograph by the Author, taken 7 March 2014.
[27] Op cit Obituary, People's Journal (Perth & Perthshire).
[28] Funeral Report, Dundee Courier, 10 April 1915.
[29] Op cit Alyth Guardian, *"A Meigle Warrior"*.
[30] Op cit Alyth Guardian, *"A Meigle Warrior"*.
[31] Op cit Alyth Guardian, *"A Meigle Warrior"*.

Private John Easson

Private John Easson, 13th Battalion of the Canadian Infantry[1]

John Easson was born on 1st October 1894[2] at Kirkinch, which lies about 2 miles east of Meigle. He was the son of William Easson, a crofter and traction engine driver from Dunnichen near Forfar, and his wife, Marjory (née Cameron) who was originally from Newtyle. In 1901 John was living at Kirkinch Croft with his parents and three other siblings, James (aged 8), Catherine (4), and Elsie (1).[3] By 1911, William was crofting at Myreside Farm (between Meigle and Kirkinch) and a further son, William, had been born. John was described as a "millwright",[4] probably operating a steam driven threshing machine on his father's farm.[5]

Before the outbreak of the First World War, the family emigrated to Canada. They boarded the SS Grampian on 3rd August 1912 at Glasgow, sailing in steerage,[6] to arrive in Quebec eight days later.[7]

They settled in Kingston, Ontario (which is situated where the St Lawrence River flows out of Lake Ontario) and lived at 138 Bay Street.[8]

The Area around 138 Bay Street, Kingston, Ontario (2014) [9]

In Canada, John found a job as a tool maker and also joined the local active militia.[10] On the outbreak of war, he volunteered for service with the Canadian Expeditionary Force. He enlisted at Valcartier Camp in Quebec on 23rd September 1914, where he joined the 13th Battalion of the Canadian Infantry (Quebec Regiment).[11] The 13th Battalion was raised as a Battalion of the Fifth Royal Highlanders of Canada, which had been affiliated with the Black Watch before the War.[12] His older brother, James, was also to join the army, but not until 29th December 1916 when he enlisted with the 75th Depot Battery of the Canadian Field Artillery. [13]

Recruiting Poster 1914[14]

Valcartier Camp – Canada. Highlanders Marching In[15]

Only two days after enlisting, John boarded the SS Alaunia to join the war in Europe, landing in southern England on 16th October 1914.[16]

SS Alaunia[17]

John Easson visited Meigle at this time and was "much admired by all who saw him for his manly bearing and fine figure".[18] His Battalion spent the winter training on Salisbury Plain, initially at West Camp South and then from 30th January 1915 at Larkhill Camp.[19]

Main Road and Camp, Larkhill[20]

In February 1915, the Battalion was sent to fight in France and landed at St. Nazaire on 16th February. The Battalion then travelled by train to Hazenbrouk, before marching the remaining 17 miles to arrive at the front line at Armentières on 23rd February where they remained until early April. The Battalion war diaries report that there was often considerable shelling from both German and British artillery during this period and also that German snipers were proving to be a particular problem.[21]

Canadian Expeditionary Force in Trenches Near Armentières[22]

On 7th April, the Battalion left the front line at Armentières, marching 17 miles from Estaires to Cassel, where they boarded buses to take them to Ypres. They arrived at the village of St Jean on the edge of Ypres on 16th April and reported that, although there was much fighting around, it remained quiet in their immediate vicinity. On the afternoon of 21st April, they moved to the front line at St Julien without incurring any casualties despite the shellfire. When they reached the front line, they found the trenches in poor state and it was reported that there were many dead lying unburied between the lines.[23]

At 4.00pm the following afternoon, 22nd April 1915, an hour's heavy bombardment began which marked the beginning of the Second Battle of Ypres. The Germans then released 168 tons of chlorine gas over a four mile front, the first use of poison gas on the Western Front. The gas affected the lungs and the eyes causing respiratory problems and blindness. Being denser than air, it flowed downwards, forcing French troops of the 45th and 78th Divisions to their left, to abandon their positions en masse. This resulted in a 4,000 yard wide gap in the front line which left their left flank wide open.[24]

This was noted in the Battalion's war diary, "Quiet all day until about 5pm when the enemy commenced a terrific bombardment and also sent over a great cloud of gas on the frontage held by the Turcos (French-Algerian troops) on our immediate left. The Turcos had to retire and this left our left flank open to the enemy."[25]

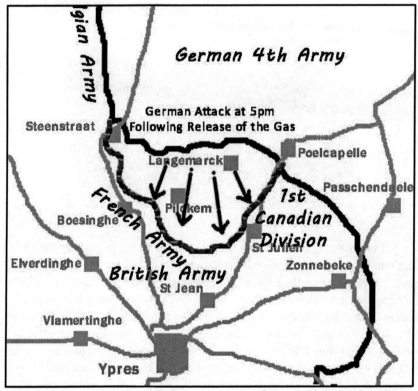

Map of the Ypres Salient Showing the Area of Ground Lost by the Allies on 22 April 1915[26]

The 10th Battery of the Canadian Field Artillery, a battery of four 18-pounder guns,[27] was in an orchard 500 yards north of St. Julien and opened up onto the German front line at 5.45pm The Battery then came under attack from small arms fire from German troops who had advanced through the lines previously held by the French. In response, at 7.00pm the Battery turned half of its fire power onto the advancing Germans.[28] It was reported that "The guns opened fire on them at that distance point blank and mowed the Germans down like flies. The lucky ones who were left ran for their lives."[29] The Battery was then evacuated using commandeered horses from the ammunition column, with many guns and limbers having to be moved to safety by hand. Lance Corporal Frederick (Fred) Fisher of the 13th Battalion was instrumental in this action, manning a Colt machine gun to defend the battery while his men were picked off, one by one. He became the first Canadian to be awarded the Victoria Cross in the Great War but unfortunately was not able to receive it as he was killed the following day.[30, 31, 32]

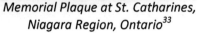

Memorial Plaque at St. Catharines, Niagara Region, Ontario[33]   *Fred Fisher VC[34]*

The 13th Battalion's right flank also became exposed as the 15th Battalion, fighting on their immediate right, had been pushed back 700 yards to the base of the Gravenstafel Ridge. The 15th Battalion suffered 647 casualties as a result, the greatest single-battle loss of any Canadian Battalion for the entire war.[35]

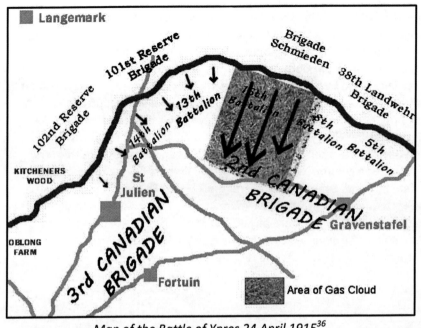

Langemark

101st Reserve Brigade

102nd Reserve Brigade

13th Battalion

14th Battalion

76th Battalion

Brigade Schmieden

38th Landwehr Brigade

28th Battalion

5th Battalion

KITCHENERS WOOD

St Julien

2nd CANADIAN BRIGADE

Gravenstafel

OBLONG FARM

3rd CANADIAN BRIGADE

Fortuin

Area of Gas Cloud

Map of the Battle of Ypres 24 April 1915[36]

The following day, 23rd April 1915, the 13th Battalion, under the command of Major V.C. Buchanan, was subjected to shelling and gas attacks throughout the day and they were forced to evacuate their trenches, which was achieved without incurring any further casualties. However, their position remained vulnerable, as they were at the apex of a small salient and subjected to incessant fire from many directions. However, their numbers had been strengthened with the arrival of a reinforcing Company from the Buffs[37] (Royal East Kent Regiment[38]).

On the morning of 24th, the Germans carried out a further gas attack. The 13th Battalion escaped the worst of the gas, but the shellfire was so intense that their trenches could not be maintained and two of their machine guns were buried and could not be recovered.[39] The Battalion was compelled to withdraw once again to the reserve trenches, with many men being captured or killed during the fighting withdrawal. The same afternoon, the Battalion was also shelled out of these reserve trenches and forced to retire further into the G.H.Q. Trenches.[40] It was some time among these desperate actions on the 24th April that John Easson met his death. His body was never recovered.[41]

The St Julien Memorial, "The Brooding Soldier", now stands to commemorate the Canadian First Division's participation in the Second Battle of Ypres, which included the defence against the first poison gas attacks along the Western Front. In the 48 crucial hours that they held the line, 6,035 Canadians - or one man in every three who went into battle - became casualties; of that number, approximately 2,000 (or one man in every nine) were killed.[42]

"The Brooding Soldier", St Julien Memorial[43]

References
[1] Alyth Guardian, *PVT JOHN EASSON*, 25 August 1916.

[2] Canadian Over-seas Expeditionary Force Attestation Paper, *John Easson*, RG 150, Accession 1992-93/166, Box 2806 – 10 Item Number:373539, Library and Archives Canada.

[3] 1901 census, 31 March 1901, *Nevay; ED: 3*; Page: *4*; Line: *15*; Roll: *CSSCT1901_105*.

[4] 1911 census, 2 April 1911, 1911 379/00 001/00 005.

[5] People's Journal (Stirling and Perth edition), *MEIGLE*, 30 June 1917.

[6] Canada Passenger Lists, 1881-1922, *Quebec, QC > Aug 1912 > Grampian > image 15 of 22*, National Archives of Canada. (via FamilySearch website, https://familysearch.org/pal:/MM9.3.1/TH-266-12410-13229-35?cc=1823240 : accessed 02 Sep 2014).

[7] Canada Passenger Lists, 1881-1922, *Quebec, QC > Aug 1912 > Grampian > image 1 of 22*, National Archives of Canada. (via FamilySearch website (https://familysearch.org/pal:/MM9.3.1/TH-266-12410-12964-77?cc=1823240&wc=MXDX-5ZS:981985501,982036101,982029601 : accessed 02 Sep 2014).

[8] Op cit Attestation Paper, *John Easson*.

[9] Google Maps, Streetview of 138 Bay Street Kingston, Ontario, https://www.google.co.uk/maps/place/138+Bay+St/@44.235798,-76.486822,3a,90y,231.99h,90.18t/data=!3m4!1e1!3m2!1s7TJB_Vub6x3rOJPKkoaYVQ!2e0!4m2!3m1!1s0x4cd2abab0399d821:0x7cab4959bfea6b3e!6m1!1e1, Accessed 22 April 2014.

[10] Op cit Attestation Paper, *John Easson*.

[11] Op cit Attestation Paper, *John Easson*.

[12] Martin, Stuart, *The Story of the Thirteenth Battalion, The Royal Highlanders of Canada 1914 – 1917*, Canadian War records office, not dated, p1.

[13] Canadian Over-seas Expeditionary Force Attestation Paper, *James Easson*, RG 150, Accession 1992-93/166, Box 2806 – 6 Item Number:373535, Library and Archives Canada.

[14] Toronto Public Library website, *5th Royal Highlanders of Canada, Black Watch, 2nd Reinforcing Company*, http://static.torontopubliclibrary.ca/da/images/LC/1914-18recruitmentitem12l.jpg, Accessed 29 June 2014.

[15] Postcard from Author's collection: Valcartier Camp – Canada. Highlanders Marching In, Valentine's series, undated.

[16] Op cit Martin, Stuart.

[17] Solem Borge, Norway Heritage – Hands across the Sea website, *S/S Alaunia (1), Cunard Line*, Copyright © Norway Heritage, http://www.norwayheritage.com/p_ship.asp?sh=alau1, Accessed 29 January 2015.

[18] Op cit Alyth Guardian, *Meigle Casualties*.

[19] War diaries - 13th Canadian Infantry Battalion 1914/10/15-1915/08/31, http://data4.collectionscanada.ca/netacgi/nph-brs?s1=13th+infantry+battalion&s13=&s12=&l=20&s9=RG9&s7=9-52&Sect1=IMAGE&Sect2=THESOFF&Sect4=AND&Sect5=WARDPEN&Sect6=HITOFF&d=FIND&p=1&u=http://www.collectionscanada.ca/archivianet/02015202_e.html&r=1&f=G, Library and Archives Canada, 16 October 1914 – 17 February 1915, Accessed 22 April 2014.

[20] Hurst War Memorial website, *Woodard, Ernest Frederick*, http://www.warmemorial.org.uk/images/pics/LarkhillCamp-l.jpg, Accessed 22 January 2015.

[21] Op cit War diaries - 13th Canadian Infantry Battalion, 16 February – 7 April 1915 .

[22] Horace Brown, Library and Archives Canada, PA-107237. *C.E.F. [Canadian Expeditionary Force] Grenadier Guards in trenches together at Armentières, Place: Armentières, France, Date: Feb. 1915*, Accessed via Library and Archives Canada website, http://collectionscanada.gc.ca/pam_archives/index.php?fuseaction=genitem.displayEcopies&lang=eng&rec_nbr=3194254&rec_nbr_list=3194254,3628695&title=C.E.F.+%5BCanadian+Expeditionary+Force%5D+Grenadier+Guards+in+trenches+together+at+Armentiers.+&ecopy=a107237, 22 April 2014.

[23] Op cit War diaries - 13th Canadian Infantry Battalion, 7-21 April 1915.

[24] The Calgary Highlanders (10th Battalion CEF) website, *St. Julien and Kitcheners Wood*, http://www.calgaryhighlanders.com/history/10th/history/stjulien.htm, Accessed 22 April 2014.

[25] Op cit War diaries - 13th Canadian Infantry Battalion, 22 April 1915.

[26] Based upon map by: Legg, Joanna, The Second Battle of Ypres, 1915, http://www.greatwar.co.uk/battles/second-ypres-1915/, Accessed 8 October 2014.

[27] Iarocci, Andrew, *Shoestring Soldiers: The 1st Canadian Division at War, 1914-1915*, p109.

[28] Keech, Martin, *St Julien*, 'Leo Cooper, Pen & Sword Books Ltd.', 2001, p38.

[29] Op cit War diaries - 13th Canadian Infantry Battalion, 22 April 1915.

[30] Op cit Iarocci, Andrew, p109.

[31] Op cit The Calgary Highlanders (10th Battalion CEF) website, *St. Julien and Kitcheners Wood*.

[32] Op cit Keech, Andrew, p95.

[33] Brown, Alan L Brown, Ontario's Historical Plaques website, *"Lance Corporal Fred Fisher, V.C. 1894-1915"*, http://www.ontarioplaques.com/Plaques/Plaque_Niagara41.html, Accessed 8 October 2014.

[34] National Defence and the Canadian Forces website, "Victoria Cross - First World War, 1914-1918", http://www.cmp-cpm.forces.gc.ca/dhh-dhp/gal/vcg-gcv/bio/fisher-f-eng.asp, Accessed 8 Oct 2014.

[35] Op cit The Calgary Highlanders (10th Battalion CEF) website, *St. Julien and Kitcheners Wood*.

[36] Based upon map by: Op cit Legg, Joanna, *The Second Battle of Ypres, 1915*.

[37] Op cit War diaries - 13th Canadian Infantry Battalion, 23 April 1915.

[38] The Long Long Trail website, *The Buffs (East Kent Regiment)*, ©1995-2014 ~ Chris Baker/Milverton Associates Ltd ~, http://www.1914-1918.net/buffs.htm, Accessed 23 April 2014.

[39] Op cit Iarocci, Andrew, p140.

[40] Op cit War diaries - 13th Canadian Infantry Battalion, 24 April 1915.

[41] Commonwealth War Graves Commission website, EASSON J., http://www.cwgc.org/find-war-dead/casualty/1591948/EASSON,%20J, Accessed 23 April 2014.

[42] Veterans Affairs Canada, Government of Canada website, *Ypres 1915*, http://www.veterans.gc.ca/eng/remembrance/history/first-world-war/canada/canada4, Accessed 23 April 2014.

[43] Photograph by the Author, taken 25 June 2014.

21

Private William Simpson Guild

William Simpson Guild was the youngest son of James and Mary (née Taylor) Guild and was part of their family of at least nine children. He was born on 13th June 1892[1] while the family were living at Drumkilbo Tile Works.[2] William's father, James Guild, was described in the 1901 census as being a farmer and a brick manufacturer at the Drumkilbo Tile Works.[3] These Tile Works operated during the latter half of the 19th century at Harryhill, between Meigle and Glamis, opposite Drumkilbo House.[4] William's mother, Mary was originally from Barry, near Carnoustie.[5,6]

Drumkilbo Tile Works[7]

In 1911 William was working as a ploughman at Mains of Glamis Farm, living in the nearby bothy.[8]

Bothy at Mains of Glamis Farm[9]

Interior of Bothy at Mains of Glamis Farm[10]

In 1912, William emigrated to Canada in steerage aboard the RMS (Royal Mail Ship or Steamship) Hesperian.[11]

Three years after William's transatlantic voyage, at 8.30pm on 4 September 1915, the Hesperian was hit by a single torpedo from the U-boat, U-20; the same submarine that had sunk the Lusitania the previous May. This attack was only a week after Count von Bernstorff, the Imperial German Ambassador to the United States, had assured Washington that "passenger liners will not be sunk without warning" which led to considerable political fallout. The Hesperian sank two days after being hit, whilst being towed back to Ireland, at a site not far from the wreck of the Lusitania.[12]

RMS Hesperian[13]

On arrival at Halifax, Nova Scotia, William caught the Canadian Pacific Railroad to Brandon, Manitoba[14] where he found employment as a salesman.[15]

Canadian Pacific Railway Station, Brandon, 1912 [16]

On 22nd September 1914, William joined the army to fight in the war. He enlisted into the 3rd Battalion, Canadian Infantry (Toronto Regiment) at Valcartier Camp in Quebec, where he undertook a short spell of initial training.[17]

The Battalion of 42 officers and 1123 other ranks sailed to England aboard the SS Tunisian.[18] In addition to its role as a troopship, the ship was later to serve as an accommodation ship for prisoners of war at Ryde on the Isle of Wight.[19]

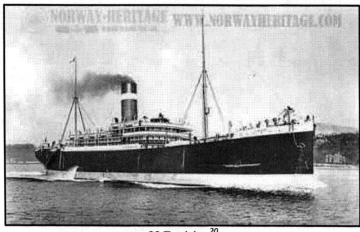

SS Tunisian [20]

After their arrival at Devonport in October 1914, the 3rd Battalion was stationed at Bustard Camp on Salisbury Plain to undergo further training.

Canadian Troops on Manoeuvres, Salisbury Plain[21]

Early in February 1915 whilst at Bustard Camp, they received an inspection by King George V. They then had only 5 days to prepare before leaving for the front, sailing from Avonmouth on 9th and arriving at Armentières on 19th February.[22] They then joined the 1st Brigade of the 1st Canadian Infantry Division as part of the Canadian Expeditionary Force.[23]

During the first week of March 1915, the 3rd Battalion was serving on the front line in the area of La Toulette, near Armentières. Even though this area of the line was comparatively quiet, the Battalion incurred a small number of casualties. During the next few days the artillery from both sides became very active, but the Battalion appears to have been fortunate, as no further casualties were recorded.

The 3rd Battalion then moved north to support the front lines in the Ypres Salient though, as a reserve force, the Battalion was accommodated in billets away from the front line itself.

On 22nd April 1915, the Germans began the gas attacks that initiated the 2nd Battle of Ypres. Early that evening, the Battalion was one of several whose command transferred to the 3rd Brigade of the Canadian Infantry to support the desperate defence of the beleaguered village of St Julien. The Battalion immediately marched 3000 yards under an escort of the divisional cavalry into the front line.

At 1.15am on 23rd April a hostile shell exploded in their line, killing five men. At 4.00am the Battalion was divided. The map below highlights C and D Companies under Major Kirkpatrick which were to defend the fields between St Julien and Kitcheners Wood and, A and B Companies further back and to the left, defending the road between St Jean and St Julien.[24]

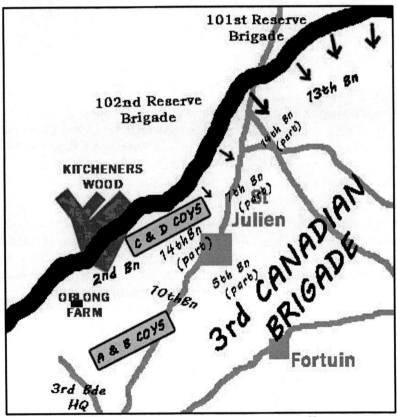

Map of the Battle of Ypres 24 April 1915[25]

Kitcheners Wood Memorial 2014[26]

The two Companies under Major Kirkpatrick became almost surrounded by the advancing German troops but they continued to take a very heavy toll on the enemy troops advancing up the Steenbeek River even though their ammunition was becoming in very short supply. However, during the morning, two small parties of men managed to reach their trenches with the ammunition they so badly needed.[27]

Throughout the morning of 24th April the orders remained for the Canadians to hold the line "at all costs". A fierce gas shell attack forced the 16th and 10th Battalions to Kirkpatrick's right to retreat and by 12.35pm the Germans had secured the front line trenches around St Julien. Kirkpatrick was then finally given the order to retire but, by that time, the intensity of fire made it impossible for Kirkpatrick's men to leave their trenches. Despite their dogged resistance, that afternoon, their exposed positions were finally overrun by the Germans and Kirkpatrick and his remaining men were taken prisoner. As a result of this action, Kirkpatrick became known as "Hang-on Kirkpatrick". After the war, he was promoted to Colonel and was later to hold the position of Commandant of the Queen's Own Rifles for three years from April 1922.[28]

Colonel Arthur J.E. Kirkpatrick, VD, ADC.
(Painting by Lt Allan Barr, Photograph by Christopher Lawson) [29]

British reinforcements arrived that evening, too late to prevent St Julien falling to the Germans but allowing a counterattack to be made the following day, Sunday 25th April, to try to retake the village. This resulted in heavy gunfire and artillery shelling all day, including over 90 high explosive shells falling in or around the Brigade headquarters in the late afternoon. Bombardments from both sides' artillery also continued throughout the 26th but, in the late afternoon, the Argyll and Sutherland Highlanders relieved the 3rd Battalion's trenches allowing them, after a considerable march, to find eventually some rest at Vlamertinghe.

The next few days were spend resting and providing support for other units away from the front line, though the shelling remained heavy enough for the Battalion to vacate their billets in the village, and seek the comparative safety of bivouacking in the surrounding fields.

The official record asserts that Private William Simpson Guild died on 2nd May 1915. However, the Battalion's war diary records 2nd May as being a quiet day with no further casualties being reported.[30] It is perhaps unlikely that he was wounded in the earlier action and died later of his wounds as he has no known grave, which would not be the case had he died in a dressing station. The official record for another member of his Battalion, a Private Charles Payne, is that he also died on 2 May,[31] though the war diary states that he was wounded trying to deliver ammunition to Major Kirkpatrick's isolated Companies on 23rd April and died later the same day.[32] It is therefore more likely, given the action the 3rd Battalion was involved in and large number of casualties incurred, that he died sometime during the height of battle around 22-24th April, but due to the uncertainties at the time, they could not be confident he was lost until around 2nd May.

Though he has no known grave William Simpson Guild's death is commemorated on the Menin Gate in Ypres, Meigle's Victory Park war memorial, the war memorial in Glamis, the memorial plaque from the United Free Church of Scotland in Meigle (which now resides in the Meigle Parish church) and also on the Guild family gravestone in Meigle churchyard.

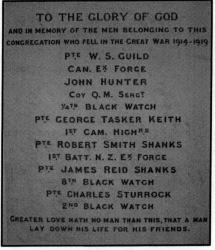

TO THE GLORY OF GOD
AND IN MEMORY OF THE MEN BELONGING TO THIS
CONGREGATION WHO FELL IN THE GREAT WAR 1914-1919

PTE W. S. GUILD
CAN. EX FORCE
JOHN HUNTER
COY Q. M. SERGT
¾TH BLACK WATCH
PTE GEORGE TASKER KEITH
1ST CAM. HIGHRS
PTE ROBERT SMITH SHANKS
1ST BATT. N. Z. EX FORCE
PTE JAMES REID SHANKS
8TH BLACK WATCH
PTE CHARLES STURROCK
2ND BLACK WATCH

GREATER LOVE HATH NO MAN THAN THIS, THAT A MAN
LAY DOWN HIS LIFE FOR HIS FRIENDS.

Glamis War Memorial[33]

Memorial Plaque from the United Free Church of Scotland in Meigle[34]

Guild Family Gravestone, Meigle Churchyard[35]

References

[1] Birth registration, *William Simpson Guild,* 1892 RD:379-, 1892 Births in the District of Meigle in the County of Perth, p 4.

[2] 1891 census, 5 April 1891, *Parish: Meigle; ED: 1*; Page: 5; Line: 1; Roll: CSSCT1891_115.

[3] 1901 census, 31 March 1901, *Parish: Glamis; ED: 4*; Page: 4; Line: 25; Roll: CSSCT1901_107.

[4] Advertisement in Dundee Courier, *TO SPORTSMEN,* 31 July 1850.

[5] Op cit 1891 census.

[6] Op cit 1901 census.

[7] Photograph by the Author, taken 23 March 2014.

[8] 1911 census, 2 April 1911, Census 1911 289/00 001/00 013.

[9] Photograph by the Author, taken 13 October 2014.

[10] Photograph by the Author, taken 13 October 2014.

[11] Library & Archives Canada; Ottawa, Ontario, Canada, Passenger Lists 1865-1935 Series RG76-C Roll T-4742.

[12] The Lusitania Resource website, *RMS Hesperian,* Copyright © 2003 – 2011 The Lusitania Resource, http://www.rmslusitania.info/related-ships/hesperian, Accessed 10/12/2014.

[13] Solem Borge, Norway Heritage – Hands across the Sea website, *S/S Hesperian, Allan Line,* Copyright © Norway Heritage, http://www.norwayheritage.com/p_ship.asp?sh=hespe, Accessed 29 January 2015.

[14] Op cit Passenger Lists 1865-1935 Series RG76-C Roll T-4742.

[15] Canadian Over-seas Expeditionary Force Attestation Paper, *William Simpson Guild,* RG 150, Accession 1992-93/166, Box 3876 – 77 Item Number: 437681, Library and Archives Canada.

[16] Archives of Manitoba, *Canadian Pacific Railway Station, Brandon, 1912* , Still Images Section. Brandon Collection--Railway Stations--CPR. Item Number 2.

[17] Op cit Attestation paper No 9790.

[18] War diaries - 3rd Canadian Infantry Battalion, 16 October 1914, http://data4.collectionscanada.gc.ca/netacgi/nph-brs?s1=3rd+canadian+infantry+battalion&s13=&s12=&l=100&s9=RG9&s7=9-52&Sect1=IMAGE&Sect2=THESOFF&Sect4=AND&Sect5=WARDPEN&Sect6=HITOFF&d=FIND&p=1&u=http://www.collectionscanada.gc.ca/archivianet/02015202_e.html&r=1&f=G, Library and Archives Canada (Bibliotheque et Archives Canada), Accessed 22 April 2014.

[19] Clydebuilt Ships Database website, S.S. Tunisian, http://www.clydesite.co.uk/clydebuilt/viewship.asp?id=3462, Accessed 22 April 2014.

[20] Solem Borge, Norway Heritage – Hands across the Sea website, S/S Tunisian, Allan Line, Copyright © Norway Heritage, http://www.norwayheritage.com/p_ship.asp?sh=tunis, Accessed 29 January 2015

[21] Curry, Captain Frederick C, From the St Lawrence to the Yser with the 1st Canadian Brigade, McClelland, Goodchild & Stewart, Toronto, 1916, Chapter VI (via http://www.gutenberg.org/files/29045/29045-h/29045-h.htm, Accessed 22 April 2014).

[22] Op cit War diaries - 3rd Battalion, 14 October 1914 – 19 February 1915.

[23] Richardson, Bob, Canadian Expeditionary Force 1914-1919 blog, A HISTORY OF THE 3RD (TORONTO REGIMENT) BATTALION Part One, , http://canadianexpeditionaryforce1914-1919.blogspot.co.uk/2013/01/a-history-of-3rd-toronto-regiment.html), Accessed 22 April 2014.

[24] Op cit War diaries - 3rd Battalion 1 March – 23 April 1915.

[25] The Calgary Highlanders website, St. Julien and Kitcheners Wood, The Calgary Highlanders website, St. Julien and Kitcheners Wood, http://www.calgaryhighlanders.com/history/10th/history/stjulien.htm, Accessed 22 April 2014.

[26] Photograph by the Author, taken 5 June 2014.

[27] Op cit War diaries - 3rd Battalion, 23 April 1915.

[28] The Queen's Own Rifles of Canada Regimental Museum and Archives website, Kirkpatrick, Arthur James Ernest, http://qormuseum.org/soldiers-of-the-queens-own/kirkpatrick-a-j-e/, Accessed 22 April 2014.

[29] Op cit The Queen's Own Rifles of Canada Regimental Museum and Archives website, Kirkpatrick, Arthur James Ernest Photo used with permission of The Queen's Own Rifles of Canada Regimental Museum. Further reproduction must not be made without permission.

[30] Op cit War diaries - 3rd Battalion, 2 May 1915.

[31] Commonwealth Grave s Commission website, GUILD, W S, http://www.cwgc.org/find-war-dead/casualty/1592699/GUILD,%20W%20S, Accessed 22 April 2014.

[32] Op cit War diaries - 3rd Battalion, 23 April 1915.

[33] Photograph by the Author, taken 21 March 2014.

[34] Photograph by the Author, taken 18 May 2014.

[35] Photograph by the Author, taken 3 March 2014.

Private Charles Philip Rennie

Charles Philip Rennie was born on 30th June 1896 at East Nevay, near Meigle, the son of Charles and Betsy Rennie.[1]

East Nevay Farm[2]

His father, Charles Rennie senior, was an agricultural labourer who was originally from St Vigeans near Arbroath. His mother, Betsy (née Sinclair), was from Errol on the Carse of Gowrie.[3,4] He was the eighth of their fourteen children.[5] The family were living Castleton Farm at Fullerton by Meigle in 1901[6] and in a cottar house at West Jordanstone in 1911.[7]

Castleton of Eassie Farm[8]

Cottar House at West Jordanstone Farm[9]

At the time of Charles Rennie junior's death in August 1915, his father was living at Pitcur, near Coupar Angus.[10]

Pitcur Farm[11]

Like many from the area, Charles Rennie junior became a farm servant[12], working on various farms in the Alyth and Meigle districts and including a period at Jordanstone,[13,14] following which he joined the 1st Battalion of the Black Watch.[15]

Charles arrived on the Western Front at Annequin, between Bethune and Loos, on 2nd June 1915.[16] The following day, the Battalion went forward into the front line where they remained for the next three days before a spell acting as the divisional reserve.

On 15th June the Battalion moved again into the front line[17] but the next day Charles was badly wounded, after only a fortnight of active service in France.[18]

Charles was brought back to the UK where he was treated in Whitechapel Hospital in London. However, he was unable to recover from his injuries and unfortunately died of his wounds on 16th August 1915 at the age of only 20.[19]

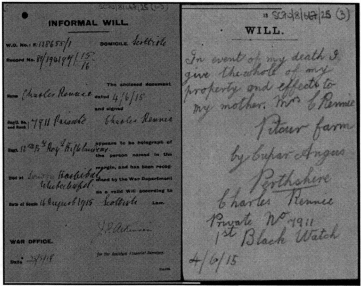

Charles Rennie's "Soldier's Will"[20]

His grave lies in the City of London Cemetery (Bobby Moore, the 1966 World Cup winning England captain is also buried in this cemetery[21]). Charles Rennie is also commemorated on both the Meigle and Kettins war memorials and also on the family gravestone in Kettins churchyard.

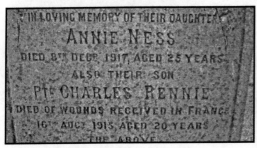

Kettins War Memorial[22]

Rennie Family Gravestone, Kettins Churchyard[23]

References

[1] Birth registration, *Charles Philip Rennie,* 1895 RD:284-, 1895 Births in the Parish of Eassie & Nevay in the County of Forfar, p8.

[2] Photograph by the Author, taken 7 October 2014.

[3] 1891 census, 5 April 1891, *Parish: Eassie and Nevay; ED: 2;* Page: 11; Line: 2; Roll: CSSCT1891_98.

[4] 1901 census, 31 March 1901, *Parish: Meigle; ED: 1;* Page: 10; Line: 15; Roll: CSSCT1901_122.

[5] 1911 census, 2 April 1911, Census 1911 328/0A 006/00 004.

[6] Op cit 1901 census.

[7] Op cit 1911 census.

[8] Photograph by the Author, taken 7 October 2014.

[9] Photograph by the Author, taken 15 October 2014.

[10] Death Notice, Blairgowrie Advertiser, 21/8/1915.

[11] Photograph by the Author, taken 5 October 2014.

[12] Op cit 1911 census.

[13] Casualty report, Perthshire Advertiser, 18 August 1915.

[14] People's Journal (Stirling and Perth edition), *Alyth Soldier Dies of Wounds,* 21 August 1915.

[15] Commonwealth War Graves Commission website, *RENNIE, CHARLES PHILLIP,* http://www.cwgc.org/find-war-dead/casualty/355388/RENNIE,%20CHARLES%20PHILLIP, Accessed 26 April 2014.

[16] Army Medal Office. WWI Medal Index Card. In the care of The Western Front Association website, *Charles Rennie.*

[17] War diaries - 1st Battalion Black Watch, WO 95/1263/3, The National Archives, 2-15 June1915.

[18] Op cit Army Medal Office. WWI Medal Index Card.

[19] Op cit Commonwealth War Graves Commission website, *RENNIE, CHARLES PHILLIP*

[20] National Archives, Soldiers Will, *16/08/1915 Rennie, Charles [Regiment BACK WATCH (ROYAL HIGHLANDERS)].*

[21] The City of London website, *Things to do, Green spaces, Cemetery and Crematorium, About Us,* http://www.cityoflondon.gov.uk/things-to-do/green-spaces/cemetery-and-crematorium/about-us/Pages/About%20Us.aspx, Accessed 26 April 2014.

[22] Photograph by the Author, taken 23 March 2014.

[23] Photograph by the Author, taken 23 March 2014.

37

Private David Alexander Lindsay

Private David Alexander Lindsay
9th (Pioneer) Btn, Gordon Highlanders[1]

David Alexander Lindsay was the son of James Alexander and Rose Ann (née Myles) Lindsay of Kirriemuir and was born on 8th February 1896 at Duthie's Row in the Southmuir area of the town.[2] He had an older half brother Peter Crichton Myles, Rose Ann's illegitimate son,[3] who appears to have been brought up with the rest of the family under the name of Peter Crichton. While living in Kirriemuir, James and Rose Ann had a son, James, prior to David's birth in 1896, followed by two further sons, Robert and William. Except for a brief spell at Lundie, during which they had a daughter, Matilda,[4] the family continued to live in Kirriemuir, where they had a further daughter, Jane. In the early 1900s they moved to Meigle and had a further son and daughter, Charles and Maggie.

At the time of the 1911 census they were living at Kirkton of Nevay[5] but, by David's death, James and Rose Ann had moved again to Hill of Hallyards.[6]

Kirkton of Nevay[7]

Hill of Hallyards[8]

David's half-brother, Peter Crichton, joined the 2nd Battalion, Black Watch on the 20 January 1908 as part of a large intake enlisting at The Curragh (in County Kildare, Ireland). Peter's name appears on the enlistment record immediately before that of Frederick Baxter,[9] who is commemorated on the Meigle War Memorial with David Lindsay. Peter was serving in India at the 1911 census.[10]

By 1915, Peter, James, David and Robert were all serving in the army. James was serving as a lance corporal in the 126th Company of the Army Service Corps. David joined the 9th (Pioneer) Battalion of the Gordon Highlanders[11] which were part of the K2 Army Group of Kitchener's "New Army" of volunteers.[12] The Battalion was formed from surplus personnel of the 8th Battalion (9th Division) and a draft of 400 recruits from the depot. The Battalion went from Aldershot to Haslemere then in February 1915 became divisional pioneers based at Perham Down[13] until going to France in July 1915.[14] Robert enlisted into the 8th Battalion, Black Watch at the outbreak of war in August 1914 but was wounded in his right hand while serving in France in July 1916.[15]

Private Peter Crichton
2nd Btn, Black Watch[16]

Lance Corporal James Lindsay
126th Company, ASC[17]

Private Robert Lindsay
8th Btn, Black Watch[18]

40

On 25th September 1915, the British launched an offensive to take the coal mining town of Loos-en-Gohelle which lies three miles north-west of Lens. In the centre of this assault was the 15th (Scottish) Division, of which David Lindsay's 9th (Pioneer) Battalion was a part. The 9th (Pioneer) Battalion was divided into four Companies ("C", "E", "F" and "H") together with a machine gun section.[19]

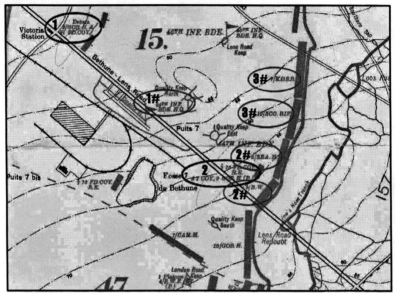

Map of the Position of the Troops of the 15th Infantry Brigade on the Morning of the Battle of Loos, 25th September 1915[20]

The above map shows the position of these Companies prior to the beginning of the action in the early hours of the opening day of the battle[21]. "E" and "F" Companies are shown as "detnts 9/GOR H" (labelled "1") and were associated with the 44th Brigade headquarters at "Quality Street" which was established a little further along the Bethune-Lens road (labelled "1#"). "C" Company and the machine gun section were near the front line by the Bethune-Lens road and are shown as "GOR H (P)" (labelled "2"). They were to support the first line assault troops of the 9th Black Watch and 6th Seaforth Highlanders of the 44th Brigade ("2#"). "H" Company were located a little further to the north (not shown on map) and were to support the 10th Scottish Rifles and the 7th Kings Own Scottish Regiment of the 46th Brigade ("3#").[22]

The initial assault was preceded by four days of incessant heavy shelling, which had successfully created several gaps in the German wire. Before the initial assault, gas shells were used extensively against the German front line but, because there was little wind, the gas clouds were slow to disperse and so the attack had to be delayed. Despite allowing more time for the gas to disperse, pockets of gas remained in some hollows and these inflicted a number of losses among the advancing troops during the attack. The leading troops emerged from Russian saps (covered trenches that were effectively shallow tunnels that projected forward from the front line trenches). These provided cover for at least part of the 200 yards between the British and German front line trenches. Some cover was then provided by the gas and smoke, but after about 40 yards they emerged into the clear and two German machine guns swept across their advancing line, inflicting many casualties. German artillery also opened up against the advancing British troops.[23]

As supporting troops, David Lindsay's Battalion was not directly involved in this first assault. However they were soon to be involved in the action. Even before the leading troops of the Black Watch had taken the front line of German trenches, 11 Platoon of "C" Company, who were initially in the 6th of 7th line, saw that the left flank of the Black Watch was exposed and so veered to the left. This put them in the front line and they successfully took some German trenches in their advance. The machine gun section was also involved in firing on the Lens Road Redoubt.

All of "C" and "H" Companies were involved in the front line during the assault on Loos itself. The Lieutenant of 11 Platoon of "C" Company was killed while under heavy German fire but, with the assistance of a Cameron Highlander who had 3 bombs (hand-grenades), the Platoon took a house in the village, capturing 50 Germans in the process. 12 Platoon lost 12 men in supporting the Seaforths, who were held up at the wire some 300 yards from Loos. The remaining platoons of "C" Company dug saps (trenches projecting into No Man's Land) from the new front line, losing 20% of their men in the process. Meanwhile, "H" Company was ordered to advance to the fire trench by different routes and, in the resulting confusion, all of both Companies became involved in the assault force. 15 Platoon in particular incurred heavy losses in the assault.[24] However, by 8.00am, the village of Loos had been taken.[25]

Ruins of Loos-en-Gohelle, 1915[26]

The Headquarters Companies, "E" and "F", then advanced into Loos. As they were under shellfire all the way, they proceeded in single file, 3 paces apart, leaving 200 paces between Platoons which enabled them to reach the village without incurring very many casualties. In their initial reconnaissance of the village, 20 Germans were captured. The HQ was then established in the centre of the village, though shelling and intermittent machine gun fire continued.[27]

The open flat land around Loos is overlooked by low ridge of higher ground upon which the German had constructed a defensive position, the Hill 70 redoubt. The original plan had been to advance to the left of the redoubt but there were very few officers remaining to direct the advance and the troops advanced on the hill, and captured the redoubt after intense fighting.[28]

View Towards Hill 70 from Site of Lens Road Redoubt, 2014[29]

Both "C" and "H" Companies continued to advance in pursuit of the retreating Germans which left them on the downward facing slope with little cover and so exposed to crossfire from the Germans' second line. "C" Company was forced to retire when the right flank was driven back and many were lost in the resulting rear-guard action. This was also the last known position of the machine gun section, who were last seen in action at close range to the Germans, very close to Cite St Auguste. They were almost the last to retire and were seen attempting to withdraw with their guns dismantled. No bodies of anyone from this section were ever recovered.

"C" Company attempted to defend the redoubt but were unable to hold it against the counterattacking Germans. At 5.00pm, "C" Company was ordered to retire. Later on, when the Company reached the Brigade Headquaters, now back at Quality Street, the roll call showed that, of the 203 men of "C" Company who began the action, 119 had become casualties. Of these, 32 were described as "missing" or "wounded and missing", mainly lost in action on the far side of Hill 70.

Meanwhile, "H" Company had dug in by the La Bassée/Lens road but they were soon forced back to a line 250 yards short of the Hill 70 redoubt. That evening they moved again - 500 yards to the north - from where they continued to provide covering fire for other units. This made them the target for concentrated rifle and machine gun fire from the Germans and at 11.00 the following morning they were forced to withdraw yet again after incurring many casualties.[30]

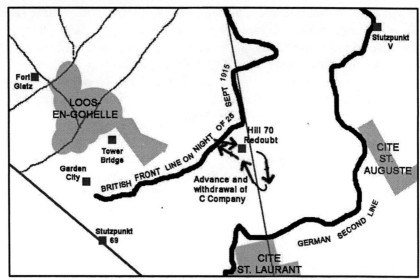

Map of the Advance through, and Withdrawal from, Hill 70,
25th September 1915[31]

By the end of the afternoon the Headquarters were forced to withdraw from Loos, which was described in the war diary as being, "a perfect hell of shell and machine gun fire, all streets from the North being enfiladed".[32]

Loos-en-Gohelle[33]

The Battalion incurred a total of 284 casualties; 4 officers and 177 other ranks killed, 4 officers and 44 other ranks wounded, 33 missing but believed to have been killed and a further 22 men missing.[34] Among these who died was David Lindsay. It is not known in which part of the above action he was killed although, as his body was never recovered, it is probable he was in the fighting at or beyond the Hill 70 redoubt. He is commemorated on the Loos memorial as well as on the Meigle War Memorial.

Another man local to the Meigle area, George Gray, who was serving with the 1st Battalion Black Watch, was also killed during the same action on the same day, 25 September 1915. George was the son of Francis William Grant Gray and his wife, Jane (née Barrie) , of Slieveview, Ruthven. George Gray has no known grave and is also commemorated on the Loos Memorial.[35]

References

[1] People's Journal (Stirling and Perth edition), 14 August 1915.

[2] Birth registration, *David Alexander Lindsay, 1896 RD:299-*,1896 Births in the Parish of Kirriemuir in the County of Forfar, p 10.

[3] Birth registration, *Peter Crichton Myles*, (Statutory Births 299/00 0133),1890 Births in the Parish of Kirriemuir in the County of Forfar, p 45.

[4] 1901 census, 31 March 1901, *Parish: Lundie; ED: 2; Page: 2; Line: 1*; Roll: *CSSCT1901_109*.

[5] 1911 census, 2 April 1911, 1911 284/00 003/00 004.

[6] Commonwealth War Graves Commission website, *LINDSAY, DAVID ALEXANDER*, http://www.cwgc.org/find-war-dead/casualty/734208/LINDSAY,%20DAVID%20ALEXANDER, Accessed 27 April 2014.

[7] Photograph by the Author, taken 7 October 2014.

[8] Photograph by the Author, taken 22 March 2014.

[9] Black Watch Departmental Roll Books Regimental Numbers, Museum of the Black Watch Archive.

[10] 1911 census, 2 April 1911, Class: RG14; Piece: 34987; Page: 8.

[11] Op cit Commonwealth War Graves Commission website, *LINDSAY, DAVID ALEXANDER*.

[12] Baker, Chris, The Long Long Trail website, *The Gordon Highlanders*, ©1995-2014 ~ Chris Baker/Milverton Associates Ltd ~ All Rights Reserved, http://www.1914-1918.net/gordon.htm, Accessed 23 April 2014.

[13] Falls, Cyril, *The Life of a Regiment Volume IV: The Gordon Highlanders in the First World War 1914-1919*, Aberdeen University Press, 1958, p54.

[14] WWI Medal Index Cards, *David Lindsay, Gordon Highlanders, Regtl No S/6339* .

[15] Alyth Guardian, *Meigle Sergeant in Hospital*, 28 August 1916.

[16] Op cit People's Journal (Stirling and Perth edition), 14 August 1915.

[17] Op cit People's Journal (Stirling and Perth edition), 14 August 1915.

[18] Op cit People's Journal (Stirling and Perth edition), 14 August 1915.

[19] War diaries - Divisional Troops: 9 Battalion Gordon Highlanders (Pioneers), WO 95/1929/1, *Report from Col W A Scott CB to 15th Division HQ on "part taken by the Battalion under my command in the fighting which took place round LOOS on 25th, 26th and 27th September 1915"*, The National Archives, 24 April 1915.

[20] Reed, Paul, Old Front Line website, *Map of attack area of 15th (Scottish) Division on 25th September 1915*, ©Paul Reed, http://battlefields1418.50megs.com/15div.jpg, Accessed 27 April 2014.

[21] Op cit Reed, Paul, Old Front Line website, *Map of attack area of 15th (Scottish) Division on 25th September 1915*.

[22] Op cit War diaries - Divisional Troops: 9 Battalion Gordon Highlanders (Pioneers), WO 95/1929/1, *Report from Col W A Scott CB.*

[23] Baker, Chris, The Long Long Trail website, *The Battle of Loos*, ©1995-2014 ~ Chris Baker/Milverton Associates Ltd ~ All Rights Reserved, http://www.1914-1918.net/bat13.htm, Accessed 23 April 2014.

[24] Op cit War diaries - Divisional Troops: 9 Battalion Gordon Highlanders (Pioneers), WO 95/1929/1

[25] Op cit Baker, Chris, The Long Long Trail website, *The Battle of Loos.*

[26] France. Section photographique des armées. Photographe, *Loos-en-Gohelle, ruines en 1915* , via Wiki Pas de Calais, http://www.wikipasdecalais.fr/index.php?title=Fichier:Loos-en-Gohelle_ruines_1915_2.jpg, Accessed 29 January 2015.

[27] Op cit War diaries - Divisional Troops: 9 Battalion Gordon Highlanders (Pioneers), WO 95/1929/1.

[28] Op cit Baker, Chris, The Long Long Trail website, *The Battle of Loos.*

[29] Photograph by the Author, taken 6 June 2014.

[30] Op cit War diaries - Divisional Troops: 9 Battalion Gordon Highlanders (Pioneers), WO 95/1929/1.

[31] Map based upon WebMatters, Carte de Route First World War website, *Loos 25th September 1915,* http://www.webmatters.net/txtpat/images/3337.png, accessed 27 April 2014.

[32] Op cit War diaries - Divisional Troops: 9 Battalion Gordon Highlanders (Pioneers), WO 95/1929/1.

[33] Postcard from Author's collection: *161. La Grande Guerre 1914-15-16 LOOS (P-de-C) – Aspect d'une rue après la victoire des Alliés. Visé Paris 161 A.Rr.*, A Richard 84, Faub. de Temple – Paris.

[34] Op cit War diaries - Divisional Troops: 9 Battalion Gordon Highlanders (Pioneers), WO 95/1929/1.

[35] Commonwealth War Graves Commission website, *GRAY, GEORGE,* http://www.cwgc.org/find-war-dead/casualty/1764107/GRAY,%20GEORGE, Accessed 26 April 2014.

Lance Corporal George Smith

Lance Corporal George Smith
1/3rd Scottish Horse Yeomanry[1]

George Smith was born at Hilton of Guthrie Cottage at Guthrie, near Forfar in Angus, on 1st February 1891.[2] He was the son of John Smith (who was known as James)[3], a cattleman from Auchterhouse and his wife, Jane (née Heron[4]), who was from Kirriemuir.[5]

Hilton of Guthrie Farm[6]

The couple had seven children of whom George was the only boy.[7] The family had moved to East Camno, Meigle by 1901[8] and were still there at the following census in 1911.[9]

East Camno, Meigle[10]

However, George was no longer with his family and by this time was working as a gamekeeper on the Hallyburton Estate, near Coupar Angus, living at the Hallyburton Kennels Bothy with John Howe, a fellow gamekeeper.[11]

Hallyburton Kennels[12]

George went on to work for Lord Kinnaird at Rossie Priory, near Inchture on the north edge of the Carse of Gowrie, Perthshire. On 9th September 1914, he enlisted with the 1/3rd Scottish Horse Yeomanry at Dunkeld,[13] which was a part of the Scottish Horse Mounted Brigade,[14] in which he was to serve as a piper[15,16]

Cap Badge of the Scottish Horse[17]

In August 1915, the 1/3rd Scottish Horse Yeomanry were re-equipped to serve as infantry at Gallipoli. The Brigade sailed from Devonport on 17th August 1915 aboard the SS Transylvania[18] to the Island of Lemnos where they transferred to smaller vessels to sail to Gallipoli,[19] landing at Suvla Bay on 2nd September.[20]

The SS Transylvania was a passenger liner built for the Anchor line, a subsidiary of Cunard. She was built just before the outbreak of the First World War but was taken over as a troopship on completion. She was later to sink with the loss of 412 lives after being torpedoed by a U-boat off the coast of Italy on 4th May 1917.[21]

SS Transylvania in its Role as a Troopship in 1917[22]

On arrival at Gallipoli the Brigade came under the orders of the 2nd Mounted Division and were quickly involved in the action, suffering many casualties until the withdrawal of the Brigade in early December 1915.[23]

Scottish Horse in Edinburgh Before Leaving for Gallipoli[24]

George Smith fell ill was admitted to the Zagazig Government Hospital in Alexandria on 23rd October 1915, while the rest of his Brigade remained in Gallipoli. Unfortunately he failed to recover and is recorded as dying from dysentery and diphtheria on 2nd November 1915.[25,26,27] George is buried at Tel-el-Kebir Cemetery in Egypt, between Cairo and Port Said.[28] It is not clear why he was not buried in Alexandria like three of his comrades from the Scottish Horse, as George is the only member of the Scottish Horse to be buried there. However, it is known that a large number of graves were moved to Tel-el-Kebir from other locations across a wide area of Egypt.[29]

Given that many casualties from Gallipoli were transferred to Egypt, it may well be that he was wounded and evacuated from the Dardanelles, though there is no indication of why he was not with other casualties from his Brigade.

A further mystery arises from his recording on the Meigle War Memorial with the rank of Lance Corporal whereas his Commonwealth War Grave records only "Private".[30] Lance Corporal was not a formal rank, merely an "appointment".[31] However, as there are large numbers of war dead recorded as being Lance Corporals,[32] this seems an unlikely explanation for the anomaly. It is perhaps more likely that he was acting as Lance Corporal without ever receiving a formal promotion or that the promotion was awarded posthumously.[33]

George Smith is commemorated on both the Meigle and Kettins war memorials.

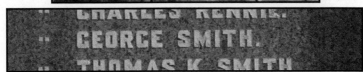

Kettins War Memorial[34]

References

[1] People's Journal (Perthshire Edition), *Piper George Smith, Meigle, 1/3d Scottish Horse (died in hospital at Alexandria), 27 November 1917.*

[2] Birth registration, *George Smith,* 1891 RD:291-, 1891 Births in the Parish of Guthrie in the County of Forfar, p 2.

[3] Death notice, Perthshire Advertiser, 27 November 1915.

[4] Op cit Birth registration, *George Smith.*

[5] 1891 census, 5 April 1891, *Parish: Guthrie; ED: 1;* Page: 4; Line: 7; Roll: CSSCT1891_100.

[6] Photograph by the Author, taken 12 October 2014.

[7] 1911 census, 2 April 1911, Census 1911 379/00 003/00 002.

[8] 1901 census, 31 March 1901, *Parish: Meigle; ED: 3;* Page: 7; Line: 22; Roll: CSSCT1901_122.

[9] Op cit 1911 census, 2 April 1911, Census 1911 379/00 003/00 002.

[10] Photograph by the Author, taken 7 October 2014.

[11] 1911 census, 2 April 1911, Census 1911 294/0A 003/00 004.

[12] Photograph by the Author, taken 27 May 2014.

[13] Dunkeld Archives, Scottish Horse Service Record Books, *G23*, p 84.

[14] Baker, Chris, The Long Long Trail website, *The Scottish Horse*, ©1995-2014 ~ Chris Baker/Milverton Associates Ltd ~ All Rights Reserved, http://www.1914-1918.net/scottishhorse.htm, Accessed 28 April 2014.

[15] Perthshire Advertiser, Meigle, 24 November 1917.

[16] Op Cit Death notice, Perthshire Advertiser.

[17] Scottish Regimental Badges website – http://webspace.webring.com/people/vr/rommel1961, Accessed 28 April 2014.

[18] Op cit Baker, Chris, The Long Long Trail website, *The Scottish Horse*.

[19] Arbuthnot, David, Dunkeld Archives.

[20] Op cit Baker, Chris, The Long Long Trail website, *The Scottish Horse*.

[21] Clydebuilt Ships Database website, *S.S. Transylvania*, http://www.clydesite.co.uk/clydebuilt/viewship.asp?id=19107, Accessed 28 April 2014.

[22] Stacke Capt H. FitzM, Worcestershire Regiment in the Great War, G. T. Cheshire & Sons Ltd., Kidderminster, 1928 – Accessed via Scully, Louis, The Worcestershire Regiment website, 4th Battalion Worcestershire Regiment – 1916, http://www.worcestershireregiment.com/bat_4_1916.php, Accessed 28 April 2014.

[23] Op cit Baker, Chris, The Long Long Trail website, *The Scottish Horse*.

[24] People's Journal (Perthshire Edition), *The Scottish Horse, commanded by Lord Tullibardine, were the last to leave the Suvla Bay sector, Lord Tullibardine having volunteered for this duty. Our picture shows them in camp at Edinburgh before they left, 22 January 1916.*

[25] Op cit Scottish Horse Service Record Books.

[26] Commonwealth War Graves Commission website, *SMITH, G*, http://www.cwgc.org/find-war-dead/casualty/474067/SMITH,G, Accessed 28 April 2014.

[27] Op cit Death notice, Perthshire Advertiser.

[28] Op cit Commonwealth War Graves Commission website, *SMITH, G.*

[29] Commonwealth War Graves Commission website, *TEL EL KEBIR WAR MEMORIAL CEMETERY*, http://www.cwgc.org/find-a-cemetery/cemetery/54407/TEL EL KEBIR WAR MEMORIAL CEMETERY, Accessed 28 April 2014.

[30] Op cit Commonwealth War Graves Commission website, *SMITH, G.*

[31] Baker, Chris, The Long Long Trail website - Great War Forum, *Soldier in the Tank Corps help needed please*, http://1914-1918.invisionzone.com/forums/index.php?showtopic=148685&hl=%26quot% 3Bdifferent+rank%26quot% 3B#entry1429886, Accessed 28 April 2014.

[32] Commonwealth War Graves Commission website, *Find War Dead*, http://www.cwgc.org/find-war-dead.aspx, Accessed 28 April 2014.

[33] Op cit Baker, Chris, The Long Long Trail website - Great War Forum, *Soldier in the Tank Corps help needed please.*

[34] Photograph by the Author, taken 23 March 2014.

Private Frederick Baxter

Early Life

Fredrick Baxter was born in Dunnichen, near Forfar, on 15th June 1890.[1,2,3,4] He was the illegitimate son of George Arthur Baxter and Isabella Addison. George was a general labourer[5] and Isabella, who was originally from Panbride near Carnoustie, worked as a housekeeper.[6,7] He was the youngest in a large family with 11 siblings, at least two of whom he never knew.[8]

Frederick Baxter (front right)[9]

Mysteriously, his father was found dead "of unknown cause" on the floor of a bothy at West Mains of Kinblethmont at Inverkeillor which is 6 miles north of Arbroath, on 31st August 1891,[10] just over a year after his birth. Following this, Frederick, or Fred as he was more commonly known, and his mother stayed in Dundee, in the home of his older brother, Charles, prior to her move to a house on the Dundee Road in Meigle.[11,12]

Kinblethmont Bothy, Inverkeillor[13]

Military Career

Fred had joined the army on the 20 January 1908 as part of a large intake enlisting at The Curragh (in County Kildare, Ireland), though curiously, the enlistment record records against his name, "Appointment from the Curragh". It is also curious that Fred's name appears on the enlistment records immediately next to that of Peter Crichton, the half brother of David Lindsay, who died at the battle of Loos and who also appears on the Meigle War Memorial.[14] However, there is no indication of how these two local men came to enlist in Ireland. By the 1911 census, Fred was serving with the 2nd Battalion of the Black Watch (Royal Highlanders) in India.[15] Fred remained with the 2nd Battalion, Black Watch until his death on 21 January 1916.[16]

The 2nd Battalion was stationed at Bareilly, in the northern Indian state of Uttar Pradesh, at the outbreak of the First World War. The Battalion was quickly mobilised to join the war in Europe, sailing from Karachi on 21st September 1914 and landing in France at Marseilles on 12th October 1914.[17,18] The 2nd Battalion was to serve throughout the war with the Bareilly Brigade of the 7th Meerut Division of the British Indian Army.

Before October was out, the Battalion was already in the front line trenches, holding part of the line near Festubert, in the Artois region of northern France. Throughout 1915, the 2nd Battalion was hardly out of action. Key engagements included an attack at Rue-de-Bois on 9th May 1915 during the battle of Aubers Ridge in which they suffered many losses[19] and on 21st September 1915, the Battalion, together with the 4th Battalion, achieved an advance of two miles despite a lack of support from either flank, during the battle of Loos.[20] During this time in France, the 2nd Battalion (which, from February 1915, would, at full strength consist of 1021 men[21]) lost 350 killed and a further 1,080 wounded.[22]

Battle of Sheik Sa'ad

While Fred Baxter and his Battalion was fighting on the Western Front, the Indian Expeditionary Force in Mesopotamia under Sir Charles Townsend had moved north from Basra to secure the important Persian oilfields, capturing the town of Kut-al-Amarah in September 1915. The Force of only 11,000 men continued north but encountered Turkish troops. In the ensuing battle the Expeditionary Force suffered 45% casualties and was forced to retreat back to Kut. By December 1915, the town was surrounded by the Turks and was under siege.[23]

On 2nd December 1915, the 2nd Battalion was despatched from France to Mesopotamia to assist in the relief of the Indian Expeditionary Force besieged in Kut. The Battalion embarked from Marseilles on 5th December and arrived at Basra on 31st December 1915.[24]

The Battalion, along with other reinforcements, were to join up with the Tigris Corps at Ali Gharbi, which was some 180 miles upstream from Basra, to form the Relief Force that was to be commanded by Lieutenant-General Fenton Aylmer. While Aylmer and the Tigris Corps waited for the reinforcements to arrive, Aylmer ordered three Indian Infantry Brigades to advance under the command of Major-General Sir George Younghusband, with instructions not to become heavily engaged with the enemy until the reinforcements had arrived.[25]

Sir Fenton John Aylmer[26]

The winter rains had arrived along the lower reaches of the River Tigris, turning the terrain, which Younghusband described as being "as flat as a billiard table",[27] into a quagmire of mud.[28] The few aeroplanes available to the advance troops were unable to fly due to the weather and being also without cavalry, the troops advanced with little knowledge of what lay before them.[29] The Turks were well dug into camouflaged positions and the two sides met on 6th January 1916 at Sheikh Sa'ad but Younghusband had to withdraw his troops after the loss of some 600 men.[30]

The previous day, the 2nd Battalion had disembarked from riverboats at Ali Gharbi. After an overnight rest, the Battalion, together with Aylmer and the other reinforcements, marched 22 miles to a point 5 miles from Sheikh Sa'ad.[31] However, the Turks were also able to reinforce their own defences.[32]

On 7th January, various units, including the 2nd Battalion, advanced the 5 miles to Sheikh Sa'ad through thick fog to launch an attack on the left flank of the Turkish defences positioned on the left bank of the Tigris. This attack was to be co-ordinated with an attack by other units on the defences on the right bank.[33]

Shortly after the advance had begun, the Battalion received new orders to attack the centre of the Turkish defences instead of the intended left flank. The Battalion was given orders to "advance where the bullets are thickest"[34] and this is precisely what they did, coming under such heavy fire from rifle, machine gun, and artillery that they failed to make much headway.[35] The attack on the right bank was more successful. This made the Turkish defences on the left bank vulnerable to enfilading fire from machine guns and artillery on the right bank and so, overnight, the Turks withdrew to the Wadi, a tributary of the Tigris, several miles to the north.[36]

Royal Artillery Field Guns in Action at the Battle of Sheikh Sa'ad in 1916[37]

Sheikh Sa'ad had been taken at the cost of nearly 4,400 of Aylmer's men dead or wounded and the 20,000 Turkish troops had been able to withdraw and regroup at the Wadi.[38]

Battle of Wadi

Despite their losses at Sheik Sa'ad and the exhaustion of the men, Aymer's troops continued to make their way up the Tigris toward Kut.[39] Aylmer planned to outflank the Wadi position and capture the Hanna Defile, a narrow strip of dry land between the River Tigris and the Suwaikiya Marshes, to surround the Ottoman force. The 28th Brigade was to attack the Wadi trenches frontally, while the rest of the troops, including Baxter's Battalion, were to move around the flank. However, as the troops had no accurate maps of the area, much of the planning was left to chance.[40]

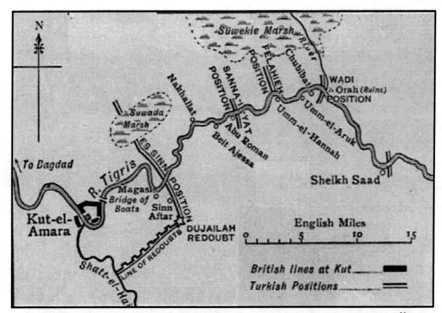

Map of Turkish Positions Guarding Approaches to Kut-el-Amarah [41]

The attack, which began in the early afternoon of 13th January, had been postponed from the morning because of a persistent mist and a slow advance of their artillery across the river. Having no proper maps of the area, the leading British column also became lost, which further delayed the attack. The frontal assault was easily repulsed with the 28th Brigade incurring heavy casualties. The Ottoman units then wheeled around from a north-south to an east-west orientation, to face the British flanking manoeuvre.

The Wadi trenches were eventually taken but at the cost of 1,600 men killed or wounded (including 40 British officers) and the Turks remained in command of the Hanna Defile, which still lay between Aymer's force and Kut. [42]

Battle of Hanna

One week later, Aylmer launched a fresh attack on the Hanna Defile. The attack was preceded by short artillery bombardments at noon on 20th January[43] and from 7.45am the following morning.[44]

Four thousand troops of 7th Division, including Fred Baxter's 2nd Battalion, advanced under cover of the bombardment.[45] The 2nd Battalion advanced and lay down 100 yards short of the Turkish front line. When the bombardment lifted, the Battalion rushed forward to capture the enemy's position "with the bayonet" but suffered many casualties from gunfire from carefully sited machine gun positions.[46]

The Battalion cleared its own front by using "bombs" (hand grenades) but the Turks regrouped at their 2nd line and kept up heavy rifle fire from their left flank.[47] Although supporting troops were sent forward, they lost their direction whilst under heavy fire and failed to reach their objective. The Battalion held their position for about an hour and a half but, as their supply of grenades was dwindling and they were increasingly coming under bombing from both of the enemy's flanks as a result of Turkish counter attacks, the Battalion was forced to retire[48]. Two Turkish machine guns had been captured and had been used against the enemy for some time before being put out of action and abandoned for the withdrawal.

The retirement took place about 10.15am across open ground that was flooded from torrential rain, during which further casualties were incurred from the Turkish gunfire.[49]

Around 60% of the attacking British force was lost,[50] with Fred Baxter being recorded as "missing" in the attack[51] along with 2,700 other casualties. No ground was gained.[52]

Nine hundred and fifty men of the Black Watch Regiment had landed in Mesopotamia on the final day of 1915. However, when the muster was called following the three battles of Sheik Sa'ad, Wadi and Hanna, only 99 men remained.[53]

Memorial

Fred Baxter has no known grave but he is commemorated on the Basra Memorial, along with more than 40,500 members of the Commonwealth forces who died in the operations in Mesopotamia from the autumn of 1914 to the end of August 1921. The memorial had been located in a naval dockyard 8km north of Basra but was moved in 1997 by the decree of Saddam Hussein some 32km into the desert, to an area which was to be a major battleground during the First Gulf War (1990-91).[54]

Basra Memorial[55]

References

[1] 1881 census, 3 April 1881, *Parish: Dunnichen; ED: 2*; Page: 10; Line: 24; Roll: CSSCT1891_98.

[2] 1901 census, 31 March 1901, *Parish: Dundee; ED: 14*; Page: 1; Line: 4; Roll: CSSCT1901_100.

[3] Family tree posted on ancestry.co.uk by "jeezie_peeps" and related correspondence.

[4] Birth registration, *Frederick Baxter*, 1890 RD:283-, 1890 Births in the Parish of Dunnichen in the County of Forfar, p 6.

[5] Birth registration, *Frederick Baxter*.

[6] Op cit census, 3 April 1881.

[7] Op cit 1901 census.

[8] Op cit Family tree posted on ancestry.co.uk by "jeezie_peeps" and related correspondence.

[9] Baxter Steve, Photograph from private collection.

[10] Death registration, *1891 deaths in the District of Inverkeillor in the County of Forfar*, p4.

[11] Op cit Family tree posted on ancestry.co.uk by "jeezie_peeps" and related correspondence

[12] 1911 census, 2 April 1911, Census 1911 391/00 002/00 001.

[13] Baxter Steve, *Kinblethmont Bothy*, Photograph from private collection.

[14] Black Watch Departmental Roll Books Regimental Numbers, Museum of the Black Watch Archive .

[15] 1911 census, 2 April 1911, Class: RG14; Piece: 34987; Page: 8.

[16] Commonwealth War Grave s Commission website, *BAXTER,F* , http://www.cwgc.org/find-war-dead/casualty/1655396/BAXTER,F, Accessed 29 April 2014.

[17] The Wartime Memories Project - The Great War, *2nd Battalion, The Black Watch*, http://www.wartimememoriesproject.com/greatwar/allied/blackwatch2-gw.php, Accessed 29 April 2014.

[18] Kerr, Iain, Rootsweb website contribution, *Re: [WW1] WW1 Soldiers Who Died CD/Lookup*, Fri, 01 Mar 2002 04:55:29 +0000, http://archiver.rootsweb.ancestry.com/th/read/GREATWAR/2002-02/1014958529, Accessed 29 April 2014.

[19] Blampied, Captain H John, *With a Highland Regiment in Mesopotamia The 2nd Battalion, The Black Watch in Iraq During the First World War 1916-17*, ©2010 Oakpast Ltd. Leonaur, 2010, p11.

[20] Op cit Blampied, p12.

[21] Baker, Chris, The Long Long Trail website, *The infantry battalion*, ©1995-2014 ~ Chris Baker/Milverton Associates Ltd ~ All Rights Reserved, http://www.1914-1918.net/whatbatt.htm, Accessed 29 April 2014.

[22] Op cit Kerr, Iain, Rootsweb website contribution, *Re: [WW1] WW1 Soldiers Who Died CD/Lookup.*
[23] Henderson, Dr D.M. The Scots at War Trust website, *Iraq 1917 – A 90th Anniversary*, Presentation given to an invited audience at the Royal Hospital Chelsea on 18th September 2007, http://www.scotsatwar.org.uk/AZ/Iraq 01917.htm, accessed 29 April 2014.
[24] Op cit Kerr, Iain, Rootsweb website contribution, *Re: [WW1] WW1 Soldiers Who Died CD/Lookup.*
[25] Evans, Roger, *A Brief Outline of the Campaign in Mesopotamia, 1914-1918*, London, Sifton, Praed & Co. Ltd, 1926, p58.
[26] Anon, The Times History of the War vol. XII, *1921*, Accessed via Wikipedia, *Sir Fenton Aylmer, 13th Baronet*, http://en.wikipedia.org/wiki/Sir_Fenton_Aylmer,_13th_Baronet, Accessed 26 January 2015.
[27] Younghusband, Major-General George, *Forty Years A Soldier*, New York: G.P. Putnam's Sons. 1923, p. 288.(via en.wikipedia.org, *Battle of Sheikh Sa'ad*, http://en.wikipedia.org/wiki/Battle_of_Sheikh_Sa%27ad, Accessed 29 April 2014).
[28] Moberly, Brig.Gen. F.J., *History of the Great War Based on Official Documents: The Campaign in Mesopotamia 1914–1918, vol. II*, London: His Majesty's Stationery Office, 1923, p. 223. (via en.wikipedia.org, *Battle of Sheikh Sa'ad*, http://en.wikipedia.org/wiki/Battle_of_Sheikh_Sa%27ad, Accessed 29 April 2014).
[29] Op cit Younghusband, p228.
[30] Op cit Moberly, p224.
[31] Op cit Blampied, p39.
[32] Op cit Moberly, p226.
[33] Op cit Blampied, p39.
[34] Op cit Blampied, p39.
[35] Op cit Moberly, p228.
[36] Wikipedia, *Battle of Sheikh Sa'ad*, http://en.wikipedia.org/wiki/Battle_of_Sheikh_Sa%27ad, Accessed 29 April 2014.
[37] Anon, The Times History of the War vol. XII, *1917*, Accessed via Wikipedia, *Royal Artillery field guns in action at the Battle of Sheikh Sa'ad in 1916*, http://commons.wikimedia.org/wiki/File:Field_Guns_In_Action_at_Sheikh_Saad.jpg, Accessed 2 May 2014.
[38] Op cit Henderson.
[39] Duffy, Michael, firstworldwar.com - a multimedia history of world war one, *Battles - The Battle of the Wadi, 1916*, © 2000-2009 , http://firstworldwar.com/battles/wadi.htm, Accessed 30 April 2014.
[40] History.com website, *This Day in History - World War I, Jan 13, 1916: Battle of Wadi*, http://www.history.com/this-day-in-history/battle-of-wadi, Accessed 30 April 2014.
[41] Based upon: Mumby Frank (Editor), *The Great World War: A History*, Gresham Publishing Company, five volumes 1915-1917, Accessed via firstworldwar.com website, http://www.firstworldwar.com/photos/graphics/gw_kuttuskpos_01.jpg, Accessed 30 April 2014.
[42] Op cit History.com website, *This Day in History - World War I, Jan 13, 1916: Battle of Wadi.*
[43] Op cit Duffy, Michael, firstworldwar.com - a multimedia history of world war one, *Battles - The Battle of Hanna, 1916.*
[44] War diaries – 2nd Battalion Black Watch, WO 95/5138/, The National Archives, 21 January 1916.
[45] Op cit Duffy, Michael, firstworldwar.com - a multimedia history of world war one, *Battles - The Battle of Hanna, 1916.*
[46] Op cit War diaries – 2nd Battalion Black Watch, 21 January 1916.
[47] Op cit War diaries – 2nd Battalion Black Watch, 21 January 1916.
[48] Lake, Percy, *The Official Account of the battle taken from Sir Percy Lake's Despatch to the War Office, October 1916, Appendix 2 "Letters from Mesopotamia in 1915 and January, 1916, from Robert Palmer, who was killed in the Battle of Um El Hannah, June 21, 1916, aged 27 years – Robert Stafford Arthur Palmer.*
[49] Op cit War diaries – 2nd Battalion Black Watch, 21 January 1916.
[50] Op cit Duffy, Michael, firstworldwar.com - a multimedia history of world war one, *Battles - The Battle of Hanna, 1916.*

[51] Op cit War diaries – 2nd Battalion Black Watch, 21 January 1916.
[52] Op cit Duffy, Michael, firstworldwar.com - a multimedia history of world war one, *Battles - The Battle of Hanna, 1916*.
[53] Op cit War diaries – 2nd Battalion Black Watch, 21 January 1916.
[54] Commonwealth War Graves Commission website, *BASRA MEMORIAL* , http://www.cwgc.org/find-a-cemetery/cemetery/88400/BASRA%20MEMORIAL, Accessed 30 April 2014.
[55] Op cit Commonwealth War Graves Commission website, *BASRA MEMORIAL*.

Private Franklin Greig Robertson

Franklin Greig Robertson was born on 11th August 1893 at Barns of Claverhouse, near Dundee.[1] He was one of the large family of John and Jessie Robertson, having several brothers and sisters both older and younger than himself. His father was a ploughman from Monifieth and his mother, Jessie, was originally from Auchtergaven, an area in Perthshire that includes Bankfoot and much of Stanley. The family appear to have moved quite frequently, living initially at Auchtergaven but also living in Murroes, near Forfar; Auchterhouse; Barns of Claverhouse and Arbirlot, near Arbroath.[2,3] John and Jessie were living at Rose Cottage in Kettins at the time of Franklin's death in 1916[4] but were later living in Drumkilbo Cottages, Meigle.[5]

Rose Cottage, Kettins[6]

Franklin enlisted into the 1/4th (City of Dundee) Battalion of the Black Watch, seeing his first active service in France on 24th February 1915.[7] Due to the extent of the losses incurred by the 1/4th and 1/5th (Angus) Battalions, the two Battalions amalgamated in March 1916 to form the 4/5th (Angus and Dundee) Battalion.[8] Sometime between March and July 1916. He was then transferred again into the 1/7th (Fife) Battalion of the Black Watch.[9,10]

He is recorded as being severely wounded during the evacuation of a sap, a trench leading out from the front line trench into No Mans Land. Although he received first aid on the field, he died on 30 July 1916 before being seen by any doctor or reaching hospital.[11] However, 30 July 1916 is significant for the 1/7th Battalion, as they were involved in a major assault on High Wood on the Somme, the last of the major woods to fall in the British Somme offensive of 1916, during which the Battalion incurred a very large number of casualties.

Prior to the battle, the Germans had been reinforcing the Wood's defences. The British were well aware of this from their aerial reconnaissance but an attack on the Wood went ahead nonetheless, in the evening of 30th July.

The attack was preceded by a concerted attempt to destroy the German machine gun posts defending the Wood with shellfire and to provide a creeping barrage to protect the advancing troops. The 19th Division had some initial success, taking Intermediate Trench, close to High Wood itself. However, the mortars of the 1/7th Black Watch made little impact on their main objective, the redoubt at the eastern corner of the Wood, which continued to maintain intense machine gun fire against their attackers. The intensity of gunfire, combined with particularly accurate shelling from the enemy, prevented the Battalion from making any headway and forced them to withdraw back to their original positions.[12] A further attack by the 14th Royal Warwickshires on Wood Lane, which leads from this eastern corner of the Wood, resulted in 171 of their 468 men involved in the action becoming casualties.[13]

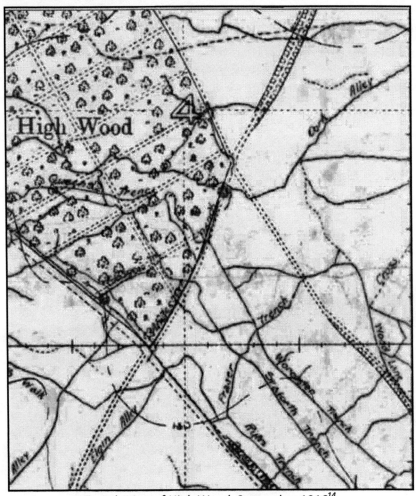

Trench Map of High Wood, September 1916[14]

At the end of this last attack in July, there were very few gains, and High Wood was still firmly in German hands, although the intense shelling by both sides had completely shattered and transformed the landscape of the Wood. The German casualties, for the six regiments of the defenders of the Wood, totalled almost 10,000 in July alone, of whom nearly 2,000 were killed.[15] High Wood remained in German hands until 15th September 1916 when it was finally taken by the British.

It was never fully cleared after the war, and it is estimated that the remains of around 8000 soldiers, British and German, still lie today in High Wood.[16]

Franklin Greig Robertson's grave is in the Serre Road No 2 Commonwealth War Graves Commission cemetery on the Somme[17] and he is also commemorated on both the Meigle and the Ardler war memorials. The report of his death in the Blairgowrie Advertiser described him as "an extremely fine lad, and greatly loved by his officers and mates".[18]

Serre Road No 2 Cemetery[19]

References

[1] Birth registration, *Franklin Greig Robertson*, 1893 RD:307-01, 1893 Births in the Parish of Mains in the County of Forfar, p24.

[2] 1891 census, 5 April 1891, *Parish: Mains; ED: 4*; Page: 9; Line: 18; Roll: CSSCT1891_102.

[3] 1901 census, 31 March 1901, Parish: *Arbirlot; ED: 2*; Page: *11*; Line: *12*; Roll: *CSSCT1901_85*.

[4] Death notice in Blairgowrie Advertiser, 25 November 1916.

[5] Commonwealth War Graves Commission website, *ROBERTSON, FRANKLIN GREIG*, http://www.cwgc.org/find-war-dead/casualty/609737/ROBERTSON,%20FRANKLIN%20GREIG, Accessed 4 May 2014.

[6] Photograph by the Author, taken 15 September 2014.

[7] Army Medal Office, WWI Medal Index Card, *Franklin Robertson*, In the care of The Western Front Association website.

[8] Baker, Chris, The Long Long Trail website, *The Black Watch (Royal Highlanders)*, ©1995-2014 ~ Chris Baker/Milverton Associates Ltd ~ All Rights Reserved, http://www.1914-1918.net/blackwatch.htm, Accessed 28 April 2014.

[9] Op cit Commonwealth War Grave s Commission website, *ROBERTSON, FRANKLIN GREIG.*

[10] Op cit Army Medal Office, WWI Medal Index Card.

[11] Op cit Death notice in Blairgowrie Advertiser.

[12] Norman, Terry, *The Hell They Called High Wood*, William Kimber & Co, 1984, p173-175.

[13] Op cit Norman, Terry, p177.

[14] Baker, Chris, The Long Long Trail website forum, *C Sap*, ©1995-2014 ~ Chris Baker/Milverton Associates Ltd ~ All Rights Reserved, http://1914-1918.invisionzone.com/forums/index.php?showtopic=163239, Accessed 28 April 2014.

[15] Payne, Dr David, *The Woods And Copses: Nature's Fortresses of the Somme on the Western Front*, (via Western Front Association website, http://www.westernfrontassociation.com/great-war-on-land/61-battlefields/422-woods-somme.html, Accessed 4 May 2014.

[16] Jennings, Alan, World War One Battlefields website, *High Wood*, http://www.ww1battlefields.co.uk/somme/high_wood.html, Accessed 4 May 2014.

[17] Op cit Commonwealth War Graves Commission website, *ROBERTSON, FRANKLIN GREIG.*

[18] Op cit Death notice in Blairgowrie Advertiser.

[19] Commonwealth War Graves Commission website, *SERRE ROAD CEMETERY No.2*, http://www.cwgc.org/find-a-cemetery/cemetery/67200/SERRE%20ROAD%20CEMETERY%20No.2, Accessed 4 May 2014.

Sergeant Thomas Brown M.M.

Sergeant Thomas Brown MM
1/6th (Morayshire) Bt, Seaforth Highlanders[1]

The Meigle village war memorial at Victory Park on Ardler Road commemorates a distinguished submariner from World War Two who was awarded Britain's highest military honour, the Victoria Cross - Lieutenant Commander M D Wanklyn VC DSO 2 bars. However, he is not the only decorated serviceman who is commemorated on the memorial. The name of Sergeant Thomas Brown of the Seaforth Highlanders also appears, followed by the letters "M.M.", which shows that he was awarded the Military Medal. The medal was award to him shortly before his death on 14 July 1917 for his service during the First World War.[2]

War Memorial, Victory Park, Meigle[3]

Thomas, or Tom as he was more generally known, was born at Nether Mill Farm, Alyth Junction on 20 June 1887[4] and lived at Woodside Cottage.[5] He was the eldest of eight children[6] and his father, a farmer who was also called Thomas, died of pneumonia when Thomas was thirteen.[7]

Woodside Cottage, Nether Mill[8]

Tom became a gamekeeper and worked for a time as on the Keithick and Hallyburton Estates near Coupar Angus[910] before moving from the area to work on the Innes Estate near Elgin and at Blackhills House at Kellas, Morayshire.[11]

Tom was already a piper[12] in the Territorials when War was declared[13] and so he was quickly mobilised into the 1/6th (Morayshire) Battallion of the Seaforth Highlanders,[14] part of the 152nd Infantry Brigade of the 51st (Highland) Division.[15] The Battalion spent 9 months in Bedford preparing for fighting on the Western Front before departing for France on 1st May 1915.[16]

Sergeant Thomas Brown M.M.
1/6th (Morayshire) Bt, Seaforth Highlanders[17]

Two weeks later, they were occupying forward trenches near Richebourg. Conditions were very poor: the trenches were very shallow, waterlogged and were not served by communication trenches. Their sector of the front line was subject to almost constant shelling, which made any movement in daylight practically impossible.[18]

On 4th June , they moved to an area north of Festubert, via Rue de Bois, the site of a famous attack made only a month before by the 1st Battalion of the Black Watch on 9th May 1915 during the unsuccessful offensive, the Battle of Aubers Ridge. The effects of the previous battles were evident, with the trenches being in poor condition and many dead bodies lying where they had fallen. German snipers were a particular problem here and had been responsible for several casualties to Tom's Battalion. However, Tom was also a sniper, exploiting the skills he had developed from his previous experience as a gamekeeper, and one of his key tasks was to locate and target his German counterparts on the battlefield.[19]

The Battalion supported a French-led offensive on 15th June. The attack was largely successful but still resulted in 140 casualties to the Battalion, mainly through shellfire, including 29 killed.[20]

The Battalion spent the next 9 months on the Somme before transferring to the Labyrinth, an area at the South end of the Vimy Ridge, so called because it was crisscrossed with many trenches. They had been warned that the German had been tunnelling in the area to lay mines beneath the British lines. This was to become evident on 28th April 1916 when between 4 and 7 mines were detonated. These explosions were followed up with heavy shelling to support a German infantry attack that was to use rifle grenades against the Seaforth lines. The Seaforths held their line but at the cost of 70 casualties, including 34 killed, some of them having been blown to bits or buried under tons of earth.[21]

On the 13th November, the Battalion was involved in their first major offensive against the well-established and heavily defended German positions at Beaumont Hamel. The start of the attack had to be repeatedly postponed, as bad weather had made the ground too waterlogged to mount an effective attack and prevented the aerial reconnaissance necessary to direct the vitally important, accurate artillery bombardment. Eventually, the conditions improved sufficiently for lines of the 152nd Brigade to advance under cover of darkness and thick mist in the early hours of 13th November 1916, with the 6th Seaforths in the fifth and sixth waves of the attack. The earlier waves were successful in taking the German front lines and the 6th Seaforths pressed on and despite meeting strong resistance, passed through the second line and continued their advance towards the village itself. However, the intensity of German machine gun fire forced the troops back to the German second line trenches, only to discover that many Germans remained in dug-outs which had not been fully cleared. The Battalion then consolidated their new front line positions and held them until they were relieved the following day. A further day was spent carrying bombs up to the new front line troops before they were able to take some rest. During their three days in the line the Battalion had lost 5 officers and 75 other ranks killed, and more were to die of their wounds over the following days.[22]

Beaumont-Hamel November 1916
by Fred A Farrell[23]

The 6th Seaforths were also involved in another major offensive at Roclincourt on the first day of the Battle of Arras, the 9th April 1917. This offensive was presaged by an extensive preparatory barrage from five days before the attack. Field artillery and 2 inch mortars effectively broke up the German wire, whilst heavy artillery targeted the gun positions, trenches and strong points along the German line. The Division also used 100 "Livens Projectors". These weapons fired 8 inch mortar shells filled with oil or liquid gas which would ignite on impact. The shelling ended with a final intense 15 minute barrage that began at 5.30am on 9th April. The shelling was so accurate that the advancing troops could advance within 10-20 yards of the protective screen of shells.[24]

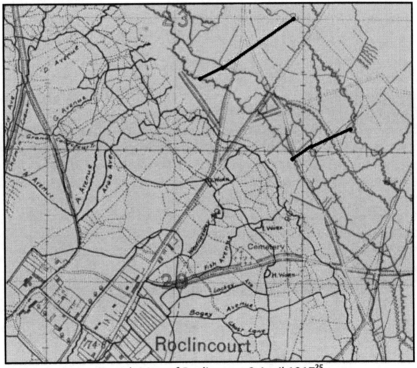

Trench Map of Roclincourt 9 April 1917[25]
(The black lines mark the boundaries of the attack led by the 6th Seaforths)

The Battalion's Companies on the left flank and in the centre took the German first line trenches with few casualties but the Company on the right was harried by gunfire from snipers. As supporting waves of troops advanced through the German front line, the right flank continued to suffer from sniping from enemy marksmen located in shell holes and a nearby communication trench, and also from a particularly troublesome machine gun position. Small parties of Seaforths were detailed to deal with the snipers, and one was reported to have taken out a machine gun team and captured their gun. We know that Tom Brown was recommended for a Distinguished Conduct Medal (DCM) for his leadership and bravery on this day, which suggests that he was very much involved in this part of the battle. The Battalion war diary records that 142 were killed, 172 wounded and 2 missing from the action on the day.[26]

Tom Brown was recommended for another DCM for his actions on 23rd April. On this day, the 6th Seaforths were to provide a divisional reserve for an attack from three infantry divisions. Towards the very end of the day, the 6th Seaforths were instructed to advance under cover of darkness to the village of Roeux where the 1/4th Seaforths of the 154th Brigade were reported to be holding the village and the adjacent Chemical Works (which was popularly known by the Tommies as the "Comical Works"). However, the 1/4th Seaforths had withdrawn to more secure positions, allowing the Germans to reoccupy Roeux. On reaching the railway station, a fierce gunfight ensued, during which both sides incurred casualties and the 6th Seaforth's Captain Petrie and Lieutenant Forsyth were captured by the Germans. Although we do not know what specific role he had on that day, it seems likely that he performed an act of heroism during this action which resulted in his commendation.[27]

Roeux Railway Station Before the Great War[28] *Roeux Railway Station, 2014[29]*

Following this action, the Battalion had a brief spell of rest before returning to the trenches around Roeux's Chemical Works on the night of the 12-13th May. While the returning men were following the railway embankment towards Roeux, a shell exploded, killing Captain Andrew Taylor and four soldiers and wounding another six. Among those killed was Tom Brown.

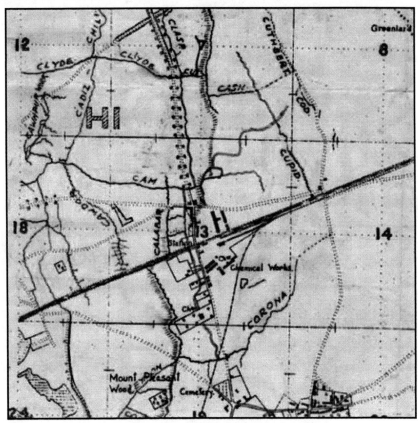

Trench Map of Roeux 3rd May 1917[30]

The paper, The Northern Scot, published part of a letter from the Battalion's Medical Officer which read,"*I am more sorry than I can say to tell you that poor Sergeant Tom Brown was killed by a shell while going in with his platoon. I should not have minded so much if it had been in open battle, but to be struck down by an unknown foe, possibly five miles away, seems always a hard dispensation of Providence. He was buried a few hundred yards from the Aid Post in a little wood, which will be a British cemetery. Poor fellow, he was a brave, fearless soldier, on whose courage and resource his company commander could always depend, and he was immensely liked by the other men*"[31]

Although Tom was recommended for two DCMs, neither recommendation was endorsed. However, he was awarded a lesser award, the Military Medal. The medal was awarded on 2nd May and so he would have known of the award before his death on the night of 12th May.

Tom Brown's Military Medal[32]

The battle of Arras lasted 39 days, from 9 April to 17 May during which time the 6th Battalion Seaforths lost 16 officers and 508 other ranks, half its strength.[33]

The map below shows a map extract from 10th Brigade war diary following an attack made by the 2nd Seaforths near to Roeux on 11 April. The Seaforths advanced over open ground into intense machine gun fire which cut through their numbers. Their bodies remained on the battlefield for some time, making such a noticeable landmark that they are shown on the map , marked as 'line of dead Seaforths' (vertical line at centre of the extract) – a chilling record of the horrors of the war.

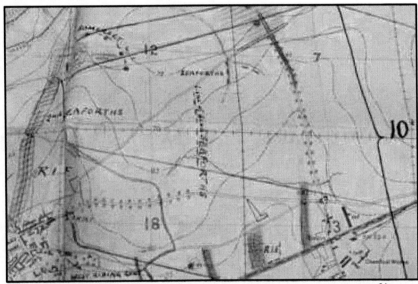

Map Extract from 10th Brigade War Diary after 11 April 1917[34]

Tom Brown is buried in Brown's Copse Cemetery on the outskirts of Fampoux and very close to the 'line of dead Seaforths' marked upon the above map.

Thomas Brown's Grave at Brown's Copse Cemetery, Fampoux (c.1916)[35]

Thomas Brown's Gravestone at Brown's Copse Cemetery, Fampoux (2014)[36]

Tom Brown had three brothers. The eldest, Jimmy, remained in Meigle during World War One while the other two both served in the army. Alexander Brown was wounded in his left hand while serving as a telegrapher with the Royal Engineers. The other brother, David, served with the Lovat Scouts.[37]

Alexander Brown, Royal Engineers
(with bullet wound to left hand)[38]

David Brown, Lovat Scouts[39]

References

[1] Paton, Tom, *Thomas Brown*, Photograph from personal collection.
[2] Commonwealth War Graves Commission website, *BROWN T.*, http://www.cwgc.org/find-war-dead/casualty/567430/BROWN,%20T%20B, Accessed 24 April 2014.
[3] Photograph by the Author, taken 9 November 2013.
[4] Birth registration, *Thomas Brown*, 1887 births in the Parish of Newtyle in the County of Forfar, p5.
[5] 1901 census, 31 March 1901.
[6] "cmosfets", Allan Family 11-2012 Family tree, *Thomas Brown*, posted on ancestry.co.uk, Accessed 24 April 2014.
[7] Death Registration, *Thomas Brown*, 1901 Deaths in the parish of Newtyle in the County of Angus, p2.
[8] Photograph by the Author, taken 22 March 2014.
[9] People's Journal (Stirling and Perth edition), *MEIGLE*, 2 June 1917.
[10] Death notice, Perthshire Advertiser, 6 June 1917.
[11] Bird, Derek, *The Spirit of the Troops is Excellent – The 6th (Morayshire Battalion), Seaforth highlanders, in the great war 1914-1919*, ©Derek Bird 2008 & 2014, Librario Publishing, 2014, p126.
[12] People's Journal (Stirling and Perth edition), *Home on Furlough*, 1 January 1917.
[13] Op cit Bird, Derek, p126.

[14] Op cit Commonwealth War Graves Commission website, BROWN T.

[15] The Long Long Trail website, *The Buffs (East Kent Regiment)*, ©1995-2014 ~ Chris Baker/Milverton Associates Ltd ~ All Rights Reserved, http://www.1914-1918.net/seaforth.htm, Accessed 24 April 2014.

[16] Op cit Bird, Derek, *The Spirit of the Troops is Excellent*, p21-33.

[17] Paton, Tom, *Thomas Brown*, Photograph from personal collection.

[18] Op cit Bird, Derek, *The Spirit of the Troops is Excellent*, p43.

[19] Op cit Bird, Derek, *The Spirit of the Troops is Excellent*, p45.

[20] Op cit Bird, Derek, *The Spirit of the Troops is Excellent*, p46-47.

[21] Op cit Bird, Derek, *The Spirit of the Troops is Excellent*, p79-81.

[22] Op cit Bird, Derek, *The Spirit of the Troops is Excellent*, p99-105.

[23] Farrell Fred, *Plate 35 Beaumont-Hamel November 1916*, The 51st Division War Sketches, TC & EC Jack Ltd. 1920.

[24] Op cit Bird, Derek, *The Spirit of the Troops is Excellent*, p116-125.

[25] Banning, Jeremy, Freelance Military Historian & Researcher website, *6th Seaforth Highlanders at Roclincourt – The Battle of Arras, 9 April 1917*, http://jeremybanning.co.uk/2011/08/05/6th-seaforth-highlanders-at-roclincourt-the-battle-of-arras-9-april-1917/, Accessed 24 April 2014.

[26] Op cit Bird, Derek, *The Spirit of the Troops is Excellent*, p116-120.

[27] Op cit Bird, Derek, *The Spirit of the Troops is Excellent*, p123-124.

[28] Postcard from Author's collection: 1. ROEUX *(P-de-C) – Avant la Terrible Guerre – La Gare*, Charles Ledieu, edit – Arras.

[29] Photograph by the Author, taken 7 June 2014.

[30] "connaughtranger", Entry onto The Long Long Trail website - Great War Forum, *Cuba Trench - 3rd battle of the Scarpe 3/5/17*, Posted on 17 May 2011 - 04:56 PM, http://1914-1918.invisionzone.com/forums/index.php?showtopic=163833, Accessed 28 May 2014.

[31] Op cit Bird, Derek, *The Spirit of the Troops is Excellent*, p126.

[32] Op cit Paton, Tom, Item from Personal Collection.

[33] Op cit Bird, Derek, *The Spirit of the Troops is Excellent*, p125.

[34] Ref: WO95/1479 10th Infantry Brigade War Diary. Copyright National Archives & reproduced with their permission.

[35] Op cit Paton, Tom, *Thomas Brown's Grave*, Photograph from personal collection.

[36] Photograph by the Author, taken 9 June 2013.

[37] Op cit Paton, Tom, *David* Brown, Photograph from personal collection.

[38] Op cit Paton, Tom, *Alexander Brown*, Photograph from personal collection.

[39] Op cit Paton, Tom, *David* Brown, Photograph from personal collection.

Company Quartermaster Sergeant John Hunter

John Hunter is the first name to appear on the Meigle War Memorial due to precedence of the rank of CQMS (Company Quartermaster Sergeant) attributed to him. However, the medal roll and records of the Black Watch only show him at the rank of Acting Sergeant,[1] though there is no reason to suppose that he was not serving in the role of Quartermaster. It therefore appears that the name of Tom Brown MM, as a full Sergeant and with a surname earlier in the alphabet, should have headed the list.

War Memorial, Victory Park, Meigle[2]

John Hunter was born in Meigle around 1889, the son of Betsy Hunter from the village and John Hunter, a drainage contractor originally from Methven. He had 3 older and 4 younger sisters but was their only son. The family lived at Melbourne House, at Loanhead on the Dundee Road in Meigle. [3,4,5]

Melbourne House, Dundee Road, Meigle[6]

On the outbreak of World War One, John Hunter was already in the Territorials and so was immediately mobilised[7] with the 1/5th (Angus) Battalion of the Black Watch, joining the conflict on the Western Front in December 1915.[8] However, due to the extent of the losses incurred by the 1/5th (Angus) and the 1/4th (City of Dundee) Battalions, the two Battalions amalgamated in March 1916 to form the 4/5th (Angus and Dundee) Battalion,[9] with which John Hunter served until his death 31st July 1917.[10,11,12]

John Hunter was killed in action at the Battle of Pilckem Ridge on the first day of the Battle of Passchendaele (the 3rd Battle of Ypres) by which time his Battalion had already seen action at the Battles of the Somme, including the Battle of Thiepval Ridge, the Battle of the Ancre Heights (which notably included the capture of Schwaben Reddoubt and Stuff Trench) and also the Battle of the Ancre.[13]

The Battalion's war diary records that the Battle of Pilckem Ridge began with "a terrific barrage" that opened up at 3.30am and that the Battalion began its advance at 5.30am on a fine bright morning. The 4/5th Black Watch was the left-hand Battalion of the 39th Division, with the right-hand Battalion of the 51st Highland Division to their left. Following difficulties getting through British artillery batteries abandoned after a previous withdrawal, the Battalion came under German 5.9" shell fire and drifted further to their left to avoid the shell fire. Small strings of wounded from the Black Watch and German prisoners were already coming down.

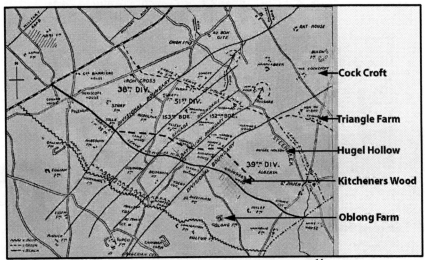

Battle of Pilckem Ridge, 31 July 1917[14]

The Battalion's first objective was to make and cross the Steenbeek River. However, the shell fire had ploughed up the ground, making it very soft and progress difficult, which made their advance slower than expected.[15]

85

"C" Company, on the right of the Battalion's advance, skirted past Oblong Farm. Field artillery had been expected to provide a covering barrage some 300 yards beyond the Steenbeek. However, no such covering fire appeared and, instead, the Company came under sustained shell fire from their own heavy artillery. "B" Company, in the centre, advanced through Kitcheners Wood to Hugel Halles (Hugel Hollow), where they also encountered "friendly fire" from Allied heavy artillery. "A" Company, on the left of the Battalion, passed to the left of Kitcheners Wood followed by "D" Company. By mid morning, despite the shells and heavy machine gun fire, all four Companies had successfully crossed the Steenbeek, from which German troops could be seen in considerable numbers at and around Triangle Farm.[16]

Hugel Hollow from Site of Kitcheners Wood, 2014[17]

"C" Company encountered heavy machine gun fire from Triangle Farm so two platoons were pushed forward to the right to capture Triangle Farm from the South East. Although they advanced beyond the Farm, they failed to take the Farm itself, despite several bombs being thrown. Beyond the Farm, they inflicted considerable casualties on pockets of German troops they found in small trenches and shell holes, and 50-60 prisoners were escorted back to the main Unit.

Two German counter attacks followed, from both the north and from the direction of Cock Croft. The Germans were full of confidence but their advance was easily halted by rifle and Lewis gun fire. Nevertheless the isolated advance platoons from "C" Company were surrounded and wiped out and the remaining platoons of "C" Company were forced to retreat back to the line of the Steenbeek.[18]

We do not know in which of the four Companies of the Battalion John Hunter served, or where or when in the above proceedings he met his demise. His body was never recovered.

His name is commemorated on the Menin Gate in Ypres as well as appearing as the first name on the war memorial at the gates of Victory Park in Meigle. He is also commemorated on the memorial plaque from the United Free Church of Scotland in Meigle (now located in the Meigle Parish Church) and on the family gravestone in Meigle Churchyard.

Menin Gate, Ypres (in 1920s)[19]

Hunter Family Gravestone in Meigle Churchyard[21]

Memorial Plaque from the United Free Church of Scotland in Meigle[20]

References

[1] The National Archives of the UK; Kew, Surrey, England; WWI Service Medal and Award Rolls; Class: WO 329; Piece Number: 1356.

[2] Photograph by the Author, taken 9 November 2013.

[3] 1891 census, 5 April 1891, *Parish: Meigle; ED: 2*; Page: 1; Line: 21; Roll: CSSCT1891_115.

[4] 1901 census, 31 March 1901, *Parish: Meigle; ED: 2*; Page: 2; Line: 6; Roll: CSSCT1901_122.

[5] 1911 census, 2 April 1911, 1911 379/00 002/00 009.

[6] Photograph by the Author, taken 3 January 2013.

[7] Alyth Guardian, *The War*, 17 August 1917.

[8] British Army WWI Medal Rolls Index Cards, 1914-1920, *John Hunter, Royal Highlanders, Regtl No 1614/240208.*

[9] Baker, Chris, The Long Long Trail website, *The Black Watch (Royal Highlanders)*, ©1995-2014 ~ Chris Baker/Milverton Associates Ltd ~ All Rights Reserved, http://www.1914-1918.net/blackwatch.htm, Accessed 28 April 2014.

[10] Op cit Alyth Guardian.

[11] Commonwealth War Graves Commission website, HUNTER, JOHN, http://www.cwgc.org/find-war-dead/casualty/1615510/HUNTER,%20JOHN, Accessed 4 May 2014.

[12] Op cit British Army WWI Medal Rolls Index Cards, 1914-1920, *John Hunter, Royal Highlanders, Regtl No 1614/240208.*

[13] The Wartime Memories Project - The Great War website, *4/5th Battalion, The Black Watch*, Website © Copyright MMV-MMXIII - All Rights Reserved, http://www.wartimememoriesproject.com/greatwar/allied/blackwatch4-5-gw.php, Accessed 10 May 2014.

[14] Bewsher F W, *Battle of Pilckem Ridge, 31 July 1917, The History of the 51st (Highland) Division 1914-1918*, ,1921, Accessed via Wikimedia commons, http://commons.wikimedia.org/wiki/File:51st_Division,_Battle_of_Pilckem_Ridge,_31_July_1917.jpg, Accessed 10 May 2014.

[15] Baker, Chris, The Long Long Trail website - Great War Forum, *4/5th Black Watch @ Passchendaele*, Extract from "*Report on the part played by the 4/5th Black Watch in the opening phase of the third battle of Ypres by Lieutenant Colonel G McL. SCEALES Commanding 4/5th Bn. The Black Watch*", http://1914-1918.invisionzone.com/forums/index.php?showtopic=106473, Accessed 10 May 2014.

[16] Op cit, Baker, Chris, The Long Long Trail website - Great War Forum, *4/5th Black Watch@Passchendaele.*

[17] Photograph by the Author, taken 5 June 2014.

[18] Op cit, Baker, Chris, The Long Long Trail website - Great War Forum, *4/5th Black Watch@Passchendaele*

[19] Gordon, Liz, Photograph from Personal Collection.

[20] Photograph by the Author, taken 18 May 2014.

[21] Photograph by the Author, taken 6 February 2015.

Private Andrew Chisholm Inglis McBain

Andrew Chisholm Inglis McBain was born on 30 November 1891[1] in Selkirk in the Borders, the home town of his mother, Elizabeth.

Elizabeth's husband and Andrew's father was Alexander, a gardener from Ayton, which is just north of Berwick. The couple had four children whilst living in Selkirk, of which Andrew was the youngest.[2,3,4] The family then moved to Newington in Edinburgh, where they had a further five children.

In 1911, the family were living at 50 Bedford Road in Old Machar in Aberdeen, where Andrew worked as a grocer's assistant. At this time, his father was a professional cricketer and groundsman for Aberdeen University.

50 Bedford Road, Aberdeen[5]

Andrew appears to have joined the 4/5th (Dundee and Angus) Battalion of the Black Watch[6] before being transferred into the 1/7th (Fife) Battalion, which was serving in the line on the Ypres salient at the time of his death on 19th September 1917[7]. This was during the Battle of Passchendaele (the Third Battle of Ypres) which lasted from July to November 1917. The day of his death was the day immediately preceding an offensive by the 154th Brigade to begin of the Battle of the Menin Road Ridge.[8] The build up of troops in preparation for the offensive attracted considerable artillery fire from both sides. The Germans put down a barrage each morning at dawn in the hope of catching assembling troops[9]. Major General Wauchope noted "As a rule this barrage fell behind the front line of posts and caused but few casualties".[10] The Battalion War Diary records that on 19th September, 8 men from the Battalion were killed and a further 14 wounded but no further detail is provided.[11] This reflects the apparent commonplace nature of such numbers of casualties from shellfire at this time.

The Menin Road, Ypres, 14 September 1917[12]

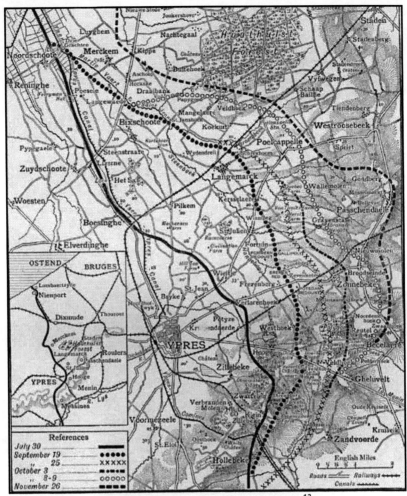

Map of the Battle of Passchendaele[13]

Although Andrew McBain's name appears on the Meigle War Memorial, the connection between him and the village is not clear. At the time of his death, his parents were living at "The Craig" at Alyth which places them in the locality but not with the village itself. One possibility is that the link may be from his father's profession as a cricketer and groundsman, as Meigle Cricket Club has maintained a high profile in the village since it was established in 1876.

Andrew McBain is buried in Cement House Cemetery at Langemark-Poelkapelle, though records suggest that that his body would have been transferred from one of a number of small cemeteries in the area within a few years of the Armistice being signed.

Cement House Cemetery, Langemark-Poelkapelle [14]

Andrew McBain's Gravestone at Cement House Cemetery, Langemark-Poelkapelle[15]

References

[1] Family tree posted on ancestry.co.uk by "dodmacd" Accessed 11 May 2014.

[2] 1891 census, 5 April 1891, *Parish: Selkirk; ED: 9*; Page: 16; Line: 19; Roll: CSSCT1891_382.

[3] 1901 census, 31 March 1901, *Parish: Edinburgh Newington; ED: 64*; Page: 7; Line: 11; Roll: CSSCT1901_387.

[4] 1911 census, 2 April 1911, Census 1911 168/02 004/00 009.

[5] Google Streetview, *50 Bedford Road, Aberdeen*, https://www.google.co.uk/maps/@57.161519,-2.109913,3a,75y,120.8h,94.84t/data=!3m4!1e1!3m2!1srHLnZ0jw6H3Y_kbJC4k5vg!2e0!6m1!1e1, Accessed 11 May 2014.

[6] The National Archives of the UK; Kew, Surrey, England; WWI Service Medal and Award Rolls; Class: WO 329; Piece Number: 1356.

[7] Commonwealth War Graves Commission website, *McBAIN, ANDREW CHISHOLM INGLIS*, http://www.cwgc.org/find-war-dead/casualty/97863/McBAIN,%20ANDREW%20CHISHOLM%20INGLIS, Accessed 11 May 2014.

[8] Jennings, Alan, World War One Battlefields website, *Battles - The Third Battle of Ypres, 1917*, http://www.firstworldwar.com/battles/ypres3.htm, Accessed 11 May 2014.

[9] Wauchope, Major General AG CB, *A History of the Black Watch in the Great War (Royal Highlanders) Volume II: 1914–1918*, The Medici Society Limited, 1926, p292.

[10] Op cit Wauchope, Major General AG CB, p292.

[11] War diary, 7th Battalion Black Watch, The Black Watch Castle and Museum.

[12] Australians on the Western Front 1914-1918 website, *The Menin Road, Ypres, 14 September 1917. [AWM E00700]*, http://www.ww1westernfront.gov.au/zonnebeke/menin-road.php#, Accessed 29 January 2015.

[13] Baker, Chris, The Long Long Trail website, *The Battle of Ypres, successive stages of Allied advance, July 30 - November 26 1917*, ©1995-2014 ~ Chris Baker/Milverton Associates Ltd ~ All Rights Reserved, http://www.1914-1918.net/maps/ypres17c.jpg, Accessed 11 May 2014.

[14] Vandervelden Pierre, *Cement House Cemetery, Belgium*, (via Hogan, Antony, St Anne's Great War Memorial, Stanley, Liverpool website, *SURNAMES F-J*, http://stannesoldswan.weebly.com/surnames-f-j.html, Accessed 11 May 2014.

[15] Photograph by the Author, taken 5 June 2014.

Private David Duncan Shepherd

Private David Duncan Shepherd
2nd Battalion Black Watch[1]

David Duncan Shepherd was born at Drumkilbo, about a mile east of Meigle, on 26th January 1882.[2] His parents, William, from Meigle, and Jane (née Coutts), from Dundee, had married on 25th July 1874 while living at 12 Ann Street, Lochee in Dundee. Curiously, both his father and his eldest brother, also called William, were recorded as being born at "Q, Sacra, Meigle". "Quoad sacra" parishes were created for purely for ecclesiastical purposes and one of these parishes comprised of the Kinloch estates in Meigle. The family lived in Alyth, 4 miles to the north of Meigle, during the later 1870s before living in Ardler in the 1880s and 1890s.[3]

Prior to serving in World War One, David Shepherd had a number of different jobs. In 1911, he was bleaching linen and cotton in Stormontfield, near Scone.[4] He later worked as a fireman on the Caledonian Railway and then as a stoker at the bottle works in Perth.[5]

Stormontfield Bleachworks in 1913[6]

David Shepherd enlisted with the 1/6th (Perthshire) Battalion of the Black Watch.[7] In October 1917, his Battalion was serving on the Western Front. On 10th October, they moved into the Cherisy sector of the front line trenches near to the village of Fontaine les Croisilles, which is to the south-east of Arras, to relieve the 7th Gordon Highlanders.[8]

On the night of 14/15th October, a small party of five men, which included David Shepherd, was detailed to venture into No Man's Land to examine a 100 yard section of the enemy wire that protected the German trenches that faced their own. The detail consisted of 2 NCOs and three private soldiers. Lance-Sergeant William Keely led the team with Corporal Albert Harry Rose, and the three private soldiers were Robert Nicoll, David Gray and David Shepherd.[9]

The map below shows the German front line (running from bottom left to top right) following the line of York Trench to the south leading to Fontaine Trench in the north. The line of wire that the party were to examine is marked by the dotted line in front of the German front line (i.e. to its left on the map) running south and west from Wood Trench to the "Sunken Road" (running from top left to bottom right).

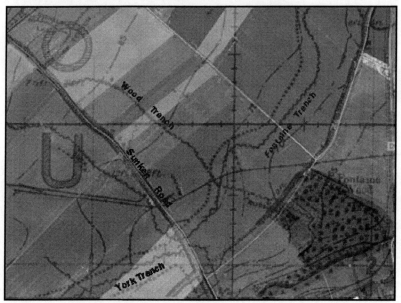

Trench Map on the Cherisy Sector, Arras, 1917,
Overlayed onto Google Earth[10]

The detail successfully completed their mission and the men began to return to their own lines with Lance-Sergeant Keely leading. Corporal Rose and Private Gray followed about 5 yards behind with Nicoll and Shepherd some 2 yards to the rear. It appears that Lance-Sergeant Keely led the group too far to the north and ran into a German sap, which was probably Wood Trench, from which a German sentry issued a challenge. Bombs were then thrown toward the group, wounding Rose, Nicoll and Shepherd. Nicoll heard Keely shouting that his legs had been blown off, followed by what he described as "a brief conversation" between Keely and the enemy in which the words "Blesse – Anglais" could be distinguished. Keely's cries then ended abruptly. Nicoll, Rose and Gray all took shelter in a shell hole but David Shepherd was nowhere to be seen.

Wood Trench Field in 2014 Looking South-West Towards Fontaine Wood with the Sunken Road on the Right[11]

Shortly afterwards, and somewhat bizarrely, Gray appears to have suffered a heart attack, as he collapsed, seemingly dead, with no apparent wounds to his body. Nicoll and Rose began to crawl back towards their own line but, as it became light, it too became too dangerous to move further and they had to dig themselves in within another shell hole.

When night eventually fell, Rose and Nicoll resumed their return journey, but were almost immediately detected and challenged by a German sniper. Corporal Rose was shot in the abdomen and was unable to continue, so Nicoll moved a short way to a safer location. He had now lost his sense of direction and so decided to stay put and wait for daylight. Throughout the following day he watched the aircraft from both sides flying overhead and by noting the source of any anti-aircraft fire, he was also able to determine the direction of his own lines. This then allowed him to return to the comparative safety of his Battalion's trenches when darkness returned once more.

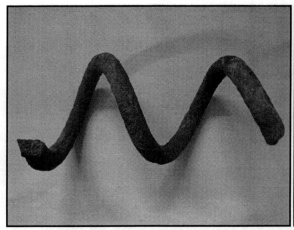

Screw from "Silent Picket" and Fragment of Barbed Wire Recovered from Close to Site of Wood Trench in 2014[12]
(A "silent" or" corkscrew" picket was a metal stake to support barbed wire defences with a spiral coil at the end which could be drilled into the ground without making noise which could attract enemy fire)[13]

Meanwhile, David Shepherd, had managed to crawl back to the front line trenches, though he was badly wounded and utterly exhausted.[14] He was transferred to Casualty Clearing Station Number 20 at Boisieux-au-Mont but unfortunately, he appears to have succumbed to his wounds a fortnight after receiving his injuries and died on 29th October 1917.[15,16,17] His grave lies in the nearby Bucquoy Road Cemetery at Ficheux.[18]

David Shepherd's Grave in Bucquoy Road Cemetery, Ficheux[19]

Following Nicoll's return, Corporal Robertson was sent out from the front line trenches with Private Turnbull on the evening of 21 October to search for traces of the lost patrol. The two men searched the area between the Sunken Road and to within 30 yards of the German sap in Wood Trench, right up to the German wire but found no traces of the patrol. They also crossed to the south of the Sunken Road but returned without gaining any further knowledge of the patrol's fate.[20]

Sunken Road in 2014 Looking South-West Towards Fontaine les Croisilles[21]

Private Nicoll's report in the Battalion War Diary notes that he believed that Lance Sergeant Keely had been killed by the Germans after having his legs blown off, though he acknowledged that he may have either died of his injuries or possibly been taken prisoner.[22] However, records show that Lance Sergeant Keely not only survived, but continued to serve with the Army, transferring from the Black Watch to the Gordon Highlanders,[23] possibly in a training reserve role.[24] He was discharged on 8 February 1919 as "no longer physically fit for war service" and awarded the Silver War Medal, an award for service personnel who had been honourably discharged due to wounds or sickness during World War I.[25] This suggests that he had not lost his legs at all, but that his cry may have been a ruse to encourage the German sentry to approach close enough for him to be able to bayonet the sentry.[26]

Private David Gray left a wife, Agnes M Gray, of Walnut Cottage, Balmullo, Leuchars in Fife and is commemorated on the Arras Memorial.[27]

Corporal Albert Rose who was from Barnsley in South Yorkshire is also commemorated on the Arras Memorial.[28]

David Shepherd is commemorated on both the Meigle and Ardler War Memorials.

Ardler War Memorial Plaque[30]

Ardler War Memorial[29]

References

[1] Perth & Kinross Council archive, Perth Library.

[2] Birth Registration, *SHEPHERD, DAVID DUNCAN,* [Statutory Births 379/00 0005], 1882 Births in the District of Meigle in the county of Perth, p2.

[3] 1891 census, 5 April 1891, *Angus; ED: 4*; Page: 5; Line: 6; Roll: CSSCT1891_115.

[4] 1911 census, 2 April 1911, 1911 394/0A 005/00 007.

[5] People's Journal (Stirling and Perth edition), *MEIGLE, 10 November 1917*.

[6] Stormontfield Heritage website, *1913 Works Photo*, © 2002 Stormontfield Heritage, http://www.stormontfield.co.uk/html/bleaching_mill.html, Accessed 7 November 2014.

[7] Commonwealth War Graves Commission website, *SHEPHERD, DAVID DUNCAN*, http://www.cwgc.org/find-war-dead/casualty/179468/SHEPHERD, Accessed 15 May 2014.

[8] War diaries – 1/6th Battalion Black Watch, The Black Watch Castle and Museum, 2-15 October 1917.

[9] War diaries – 1/6th Battalion Black Watch, *REPORT ON FATE OF PATROL SENT OUT ON NIGHT OF 14/15 OCTOBER 1917* , The Black Watch Castle and Museum.

[10] RootsChat.com website, *Curtain Trench at Cherisy, 6th Bn end of April 1917*, http://www.rootschat.com/forum/index.php?topic=649880.18, Accessed 15 May 2014 and Google Earth image of area to North East of Fontaine-les-Croiselles, Pas–de-Calais. Accessed 15 May 2014.

[11] Photograph by the Author, taken 7 June 2014.

[12] Items in the Author's personal collection.

[13] Martin G", Entry onto The Long Long Trail website - Great War Forum, *Troublesome Military Words*, Post on Apr 29 2014 08:01 AM, http://1914-1918.invisionzone.com/forums/index.php?showtopic=210686, Accessed 14 June 2014.

[14] Op cit War diaries – 1/6th Battalion Black Watch, *REPORT ON FATE OF PATROL SENT OUT ON NIGHT OF 14/15 OCTOBER 1917.*

[15] Op cit Commonwealth War Graves Commission website, *SHEPHERD, DAVID DUNCAN.*

[16] Commonwealth War Graves Commission website, *BUCQUOY ROAD CEMETERY, FICHEUX,* http://www.cwgc.org/find-a-cemetery/cemetery/17600/BUCQUOY%20ROAD%20CEMETERY,%20FICHEUX, Accessed 15 May 2014.

[17] The World War I Document Archive, *LOCATION OF HOSPITALS AND CASUALTY CLEARING STATIONS IN THE GREAT WAR*, sent from the Ministry of Pensions to the British Red Cross Society Records Office, 13 July 1923, http://www.vlib.us/medical/CCS/ccs.htm, Accessed 15 May 2014.

[18] Op cit Commonwealth War Graves Commission website, *SHEPHERD, DAVID DUNCAN.*

[19] Photograph by the Author, taken 9 June 2013.

[20] War diaries – 1/6th Battalion Black Watch, *PATROL REPORT BY No 265700 Corporal ROBERTSON S*, 21 October 1917, The Black Watch Castle and Museum.

[21] Photograph by the Author, taken 7 June 2014.

[22] Op cit War diaries – 1/6th Battalion Black Watch, *REPORT ON FATE OF PATROL SENT OUT ON NIGHT OF 14/15 OCTOBER 1917.*

[23] Medal Card, *William Keely*, Posted by McCluskey, Tom A, onto The Long Long Trail website - Great War Forum, *6th Black Watch Patrol*, Posted on 15 August 2007 - 08:45 PM, http://1914-1918.invisionzone.com/forums/index.php?showtopic=62288, Accessed 15 May 2014.

[24] McCluskey, Tom A, Entry onto The Long Long Trail website - Great War Forum, *6th Black Watch Patrol*, Post on 15 August 2007 - 08:45 PM, http://1914-1918.invisionzone.com/forums/index.php?showtopic=62288, Accessed 15 May 2014 .

[25] Extract from *Roll of Individuals Entitled to the "War Badge"*, Posted by McCluskey, Tom A, onto The Long Long Trail website - Great War Forum, *6th Black Watch Patrol*, Posted 14 August 2010 - 11:18 AM, ©National Archives, http://1914-1918.invisionzone.com/forums/index.php?showtopic=62288, Accessed 15 May 2014.

[26] Op cit McCluskey, Tom A, Entry onto The Long Long Trail website - Great War Forum, *6th Black Watch Patrol*, Post on 04 October 2007 - 11:49 PM.

[27] Commonwealth War Graves Commission website, *GRAY, DAVID*, http://www.cwgc.org/find-war-dead/casualty/636990/GRAY,%20DAVID, Accessed 15 May 2014.

[28] Commonwealth War Graves Commission website, *ROSE, ALBERT HARRY*, http://www.cwgc.org/find-war-dead/casualty/1637664/ROSE,%20ALBERT%20HARRY, Accessed 15 May 2014.

[29] Photograph by the Author, taken 23 March 2014.

[30] Photograph by the Author, taken 23 March 2014.

Gunner Thomas Murray

Thomas was born at Grange of Airlie in Angus on 19th July 1899, the illegitimate son of Jacobina Murray, an 18 year old domestic servant originally from Kinnettles, near Forfar, Angus.[1,2] Thomas was raised by his grandparents, Jacobina's parents, Andrew and Ann Murray[3,4] while his mother continued to work as a domestic servant in Airlie,[5] By 1911, Jacobina had moved to serve a family who lived on the Perth Road in Dundee.[6] She died in Cargill, Perth in 1964, at the age of 82.[7]

Thomas's grandfather, Andrew, was a shepherd from Kettins, near Meigle, and his grandmother, Ann, was born at Fowlis Easter, near Dundee. Andrew and Ann had five of their own offspring, Jacobina's siblings, living with them at Crathie, Meigle in 1901, together with three of their grandchildren, including Thomas. By 1911, the household, which still included three generations of the Murray family, had moved to Langlogie by Drumkilbo, Meigle.[8,9,10]

Thomas Murray enlisted in Dundee[11] and became a gunner in the 169th Brigade of the Royal Field Artillery.[12] The 169th Brigade had been broken up in 1916, but reformed and went to the Western Front on 14th May 1917. As 18 was (at least in theory) the minimum age for enlisting, this was presumably prior to Thomas joining the Brigade. The Brigade operated 18 pounder guns, the standard field gun of World War One.[13] Almost 100 million 18 pounder rounds were expended on the Western Front during the First World War.[14]

A Battery of 18-pounder Field Guns of the Royal Field Artillery in Action Near the Town of Albert on the Somme, 28 March 1918[15]

Thomas was only 18 years old when he was killed on 6th May 1918 while serving on the Somme. This was at the time of the Ludendorff offensive, from which the Germans gained considerable ground in an attempt to break the deadlock on the Western Front before American troops arrived in numbers.

Three days prior to his death, the headquarters of the 169th Brigade had moved to Henencourt Chateau, about 5 miles west of the town of Albert, to take over from the 10th Australian Field Artillery Brigade.[16]

Henencourt Chateau[17]

Thomas was with 139 Battery, which took up positions a mile further east on the western edge of the village of Millencourt. His Battery was providing "counter preparation" fire to prevent any build up of troops for a German attack and general harassing fire against enemy movements behind the German lines. It is not clear how Thomas was killed but he was the only casualty from the Brigade on a day when enemy artillery was reported as being quiet.[18]

He was buried at Ribemont Communal Cemetery Extension, Somme which is about 5 miles south-west of Albert.[19]

Aerial Photograph of Millencourt, April 1918[20]

References

[1] Birth registration, *Thomas Murray,* (Statutory Births 270/00 0012), 1899 Births in the Parish of Airlie in the County of Forfar, p 4.

[2] Birth registration, *Jacobina Murray,* Scotland, Births and Baptisms, 1564-1950. Salt Lake City, Utah: FamilySearch, 2013. Accessed via Ancestry.com. Scotland, Select Births and Baptisms, 1564-1950 [database on-line]. Provo, UT, USA: Ancestry.com Operations, Inc., 2014.

[3] 1911 census, 2 April 1911, Census 1911 282/01 006/00 015.

[4] 1901 census, 31 March 1901, Parish: *Meigle;* ED: *3;* Page: *4;* Line: *1;* Roll: *CSSCT1901_122.*

[5] 1901 census, 31 March 1901, Parish: *Airlie;* ED: *4;* Page: *8;* Line: *12;* Roll: *CSSCT1901_85.*

[6] 1911 census, 2 April 1911, Census 1911 282/01 006/00 015.

[7] Death registration, 1964, District: Cargill, Perth 338/00 0001.

[8] 1891 census, 5 April 1891, Parish: Ruthven; ED: 1; Page: 5; Line: 1; Roll: CSSCT1891_105.

[9] Op cit 1901 census, 31 March 1901, Parish: *Meigle;* ED: *3;* Page: *4;* Line: 1; Roll: CSSCT1901_122.

[10] Op cit 1911 census, 2 April 1911, Census 1911 379/00 001/00 003.

[11] British and Irish Military Databases. The Naval and Military Press Ltd Accessed via Military-Genealogy.com, comp. UK, Soldiers Died in the Great War, 1914-1919 [database on-line]. Provo, UT, USA: Ancestry.com Operations Inc, 2008. Accessed 28 May 2014.

[12] Commonwealth War Grave s Commission website, *MURRAY,T,* http://www.cwgc.org/find-war-dead/casualty/43610/MURRAY,%20T, Accessed 28 May 2014.

[13] "rflory", Entry onto The Long Long Trail website - Great War Forum, *169 Brigade RFA,* Post on 30 November 2008 - 07:39 PM, http://1914-1918.invisionzone.com/forums/index.php?showtopic=112088, Accessed 28 May 2014.

[14] Clarke Dale, British Artillery 1914-1918, Osprey Publishing, 2008, ISBN 978 1 84176 688 1, p35.

[15] Imperial War Museum, IWM Prints website, *A battery of 18-pounder field guns of the Royal Field Artillery in action near the town of Albert on the Somme, 28 March 1918*, McLellan D (2nd Lieutenant), © IWM (Q 8648), http://lowres-picturecabinet.com.s3-eu-west-1.amazonaws.com/162/main/2/743557.jpg, Accessed 28 May 2014.

[16] War diaries – 169th Brigade Royal Field Artillery WO 95/2349_4, The National Archives, 3 May 1918.

[17] Albin Denis, Escadrille MS23 – N23 – SPA23, http://albindenis.free.fr/Site_escadrille/escadrille023_2.htm Accessed 25 August 2014.

[18] Op cit War diaries – 169th Brigade Royal Field Artillery WO 95/2349_4, The National Archives, 3-6 May 1918.

[19] Op cit Commonwealth War Graves Commission website, *MURRAY,T.*

[20] McMaster University Library, *Aerial photo, World War, 1914-1918; Millencourt April 1918*, © 2013 McMaster University, Accessed 25 August 2014.

Private George Tasker Keith

George Tasker Keith and his twin brother, Fergus, were born on 14th November 1899 in Meigle.[1,2,3] Their father was William Tasker Keith who was born at Airlie in 1860.[4,5] In 1882, William had emigrated to Philadelphia where he met Mary Jane McFarland, who was from the Ballymoney district of County Antrim. The couple married in Philadelphia in 1885[6] and had two children: William Tasker and Margaret (Maggie), before William returned to Scotland with his family sometime between 1889 and 1891.

The family settled in Meigle[7] where two further children were born[8] before Mary Jane gave birth to the twins[9], George and Fergus.[10] William and Mary Jane had a total of eleven children, though one appears to have died in infancy.[11] In 1908, the two children who had been born in the USA, William and Maggie, returned to Philadelphia.[12]

George was working in the advertising department of the Courier office in Dundee[13] when he joined the 1st Battalion of the Cameron Highlanders.[14]

Courier Building, Dundee[15]

106

In early September 1918, his Battalion was in the front line in Picardy, just north of St Quentin.[16] By this time, the Allies' counteroffensive had retaken all of the ground previously taken during the Ludendorff Offensive, the German spring offensive of 1918.[17] As they withdrew to the Hindenburg Line defences, the Germans implemented a "scorched earth" policy, destroying all they could as they fell back. The Hindenburg Line, or the Siegfried Stellung as it was known by the Germans,[18] was a semi-permanent line of defences that Hindenburg ordered to be created several miles behind the German front lines in late 1916. Many considered this defensive line to be effectively impregnable.[19]

A Section of the Hindenburg Line [20]

On the day of George's death, the 18th September, a major battle of the war took place at Epehy, where German outposts occupied high ground in front of the Hindenburg Line.[21] George and the 1st Cameron Highlanders were at Maissemy, about 10 miles to the South, where they were involved in a similar offensive.

Maissemy[22]

The Battalion was formed up at 4.50am[23] and advanced towards the German lines in rain and thick mist[24] behind a creeping barrage of artillery fire. The four Companies of the 1st Cameron Highlanders advanced towards their first objective, Villemay Trench, with the Kings Royal Rifle Corps on their left and the 1st Battalion of the Loyal North Lancashire Regiment on their right.[25]

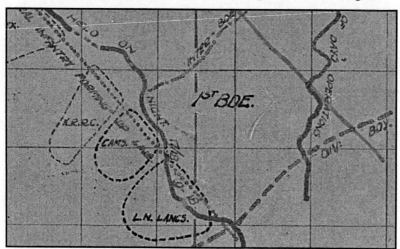

Detail from Map in 1st Battalion Cameron Highlanders War Diary
Showing Formation at the Start of the Battle on 18 September 1918[26]

There was a thick belt of wire to overcome to reach Villemay Trench but fortunately there was little enemy shell fire as the Battalion advanced. However, several casualties were incurred from the many machine guns that defended the trench, especially among "D" Company on the right. Although this resulted in some delay against the battle plan, the trench was eventually successfully taken.[27]

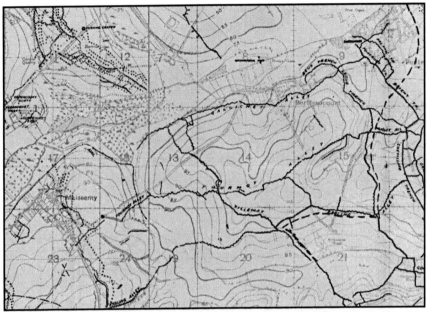

Trench Map of the Maissemy Area from September 1918 showing similar Area to that Covered by the Detail from the Map in the War Diary (see previous page)[28]

The Battalion continued to advance towards its second objective, Leduc Trench, which is just to the north-east of Berthaucourt. However, the advance of the 1st Battalion of the Loyal North Lancashire Regiment had been held up by the German machine guns and this left the Cameron's right flank exposed and slowed down their progress. By the end of the day, significant advances had been made but Leduc Trench remained in German hands.[29]

George Keith was probably a machine gunner during the attack on 18th September as his commanding officer later commented that he had been a keen Lewis gunner.[30,31] However, we do not know which Company he was attached to or where or when in the assault he may have been killed. As he was only 18 years old when he died, it is unlikely that he would have been serving in France for very long.

His grave is in the Bellicourt Military Cemetery, close to the action described above.[32]

Following George's death, George's parents and five of his siblings, including his twin brother, Fergus, emigrated to join his two siblings who were already in the USA, arriving in the States in April 1920.[33] His parents and most of his siblings remained in Pennsylvania, but George's older brother, William Tasker Keith, moved to New Jersey where he remained his death in 1969.[34]

References

[1] National Archives; Washington, D.C.; Naturalization Petitions for the Eastern District of Pennsylvania, 1795-1930 Series: M1522; Roll: 309; Record Type: (Roll 309) Petition Nos. 81491-81920, *Fergus Keith*.

[2] 1901 census, 5 April 1901, *Parish: Meigle; ED: 2*; Page: 4; Line: 16; Roll: CSSCT1901_122.

[3] Alyth Guardian, *The War*, 11 October 1918.

[4] Op cit 1901 census.

[5] 1911 census, 2 April 1911, 1911 379/00 002/00 005.

[6] Family tree posted on ancestry.co.uk by "trotter371", Accessed 26 July 2014.

[7] 1891 census, 5 April 1891, Parish: Meigle; ED: 2; Page: 3; Line: 17; Roll: CSSCT1891_115.

[8] Op cit 1901 census.

[9] Op cit Alyth Guardian, *The War*, 11 October 1918.

[10] Op cit 1901 census.

[11] Op cit 1911 census.

[12] Op cit Family tree posted on ancestry.co.uk by "trotter371".

[13] People's Journal (Stirling & Perth Edition), *Meigle*, 12 October 1918.

[14] Commonwealth War Graves Commission website, *KEITH G T*, http://www.cwgc.org/find-war-dead/casualty/238348/KEITH,%20G%20T, Accessed 26 July 2014.

[15] Bygone Dundee website, *July 1933*, Local History Centre, Dundee Central Library, http://bygone.dundeecity.gov.uk/bygone-news/july-1933, Accessed 14 December 2014.

[16] War diaries - 1st Battalion Cameron Highlanders, WO 95/1264_6, The National Archives, 18 September 1918.

[17] Carter, Jerome, *An Overview of the Battle of Epehy 1918*, September 12, 2011.

[18] Mitchinson, K W, Epehy *Hindenburg Line*, Pen Sword Books, ISBN 0 85052 627 2, 2012.

[19] Op cit Carter, Jerome.

[20] Kinnethmont website, *A Section of the Hindenburg Line to the north of Morchies*, © Copyright kinnethmont.co.uk 2012, http://www.kinnethmont.co.uk/1914-1918_files/john-stewart.htm, Accessed 14 December 2014.

[21] Op cit Mitchinson, K W.

[22] Image of old postcard, Source unknown.

[23] Op cit War diaries - 1st Battalion Cameron Highlanders.

[24] Sheldon, Jack, Entry onto The Long Long Trail website - Great War Forum, *1st Battalion Loyal North Lancs* (Extract from regimental history), http://1914-1918.invisionzone.com/forums/index.php?showtopic=82847, Posted 26 September 2007 - 06:34 AM.

[25] Op cit War diaries - 1st Battalion Cameron Highlanders.

[26] Op cit War diaries - 1st Battalion Cameron Highlanders.

[27] Op cit War diaries - 1st Battalion Cameron Highlanders.

[28] Mc Master University, 190WW1MAP, Trench map, World War, 1914-1918; Maissemy, UNKNOWN. September, 1918 - 1:20,000, http://digitalarchive.mcmaster.ca/islandora/object/macrepo%3A4247/-/collection, Accessed 26 July 2014. [Note contrast and hues enhanced from original to highlight the trench system].

[29] Op cit War diaries - 1st Battalion Cameron Highlanders.

[30] Op cit Alyth Guardian.

[31] Op cit People's Journal (Perthshire Edition), *Meigle*, 12 October 1918.

[32] Op cit Commonwealth War Grave s Commission website, *KEITH G T*.

[33] List or Manifest of Alien Passengers for the United States, SS Haverford Passengers sailing from Liverpool, March 26th 1920.

[34] Op cit Op cit Family tree posted on ancestry.co.uk by "trotter371".

Private Charles Gardyne Sturrock

Private Charles Sturrock
2nd Battalion Black Watch[1]

Charles Gardyne Sturrock was born at Smithfield Farm, Monikie, near Dundee, on 12th February 1885.[2] He was the youngest of the three sons of David and Jessie Sturrock and also had an older sister, Jane.[3,4,5]

Smithfield Farm, Monikie[6]

The family farmed for many years at Tillihoit at Carmyllie, Angus[7,8] before moving to South West Fullarton sometime after the 1911 census.[9,10]

Tillihoit Farm, Carmyllie[11]

South West Fullerton Farm[12]

Charles Sturrock enlisted at Perth with the Training Reserve of the Black Watch on 31st May 1916 and was posted to one of the General Service Battalions (8th-11th Battalions)[13] to undergo training at the Nigg Training Camp during June 1916.[14] The Roll Book suggests that it is most likely that this would have been with the 11th Battalion.[15] After completing this training he was then transferred for service in the 2nd Battalion of the Black Watch.[16,17]

Black Watch Training Camp at Nigg[18]

The 2nd Battalion left France for Mesopotamia in December 1915[19] and so Charles would not have seen any action with the Battalion on the Western Front. The 2nd Battalion saw such heavy losses in early 1916 that the Battalion was temporarily amalgamated with the 1st Battalion of the Seaforth Highlanders[20]. It is therefore likely that Charles went out to the Middle East to help bring the numbers in the Battalion back to a reasonable fighting strength.

Private Charles Sturrock
2nd Battalion Black Watch[21]

The 2nd Battalion continued to take a very active role in the actions against the Turkish forces and took Baghdad in March 1917, following the Battle of Sannaiyat.

General Maude's entry into Baghdad, 11 March 1917[22]

Operations in Mesopotamia were concluded at the end of 1917 and so the 2nd Battalion moved to Palestine, taking part in General Edmund Allenby's successful action at the Battle of Megiddo in September 1918.[23]

In the last days of the war, the Battalion was ravaged by illness from influenza and dysentery with many men who had survived years of warfare, succumbing to the effects of disease. Although the prevalence of disease in the Battalion was improving considerably by early November,[24] Charles Sturrock died from malaria on 7th November 1918,[25] just four days before the Great War came to an end.

Charles Sturrock was buried in Beirut War Cemetery[26] and is commemorated on the Meigle, Alyth and Carmylie war memorials and also on the Sturrock family gravestone in Meigle Churchyard.

EGYPTIAN EXPEDITIONARY FORCE

PHOTOGRAPH OF THE GRAVE
OF THE LATE

(Name) *Sturrock, C.*

(No.) *S/6059* (Rank) *Private.*

(Unit) *Black Watch*

Died *7—11—1918*

Buried *Beirut* Military Cemetery

Plot

Number of Grave

Charles Sturrock's Grave in Beirut Military Cemetery[27]

Beirut War Cemetery[28]

117

Alyth War Memorial[29]

Sturrock Family Gravestone in Meigle Churchyard[30]

Carmylie War Memorial[31]

References

[1] Wilkie, Irene, *Charles Sturrock*, Photograph from personal collection.

[2] Birth registration, *Charles Gardyne Sturrock,* (Statutory Births 311/00 0004), 1885 Births in the Parish of Monikie in the County of Forfar, p 2.

[3] 1891 census, 5 April 1891, Parish: *Monikie*; *ED: 2*; Page: *6*; Line: *15*; Roll: *CSSCT1891_103*.

[4] 1901 census, 31 March 1901, Parish: *Carmyllie*; *ED: 2*; Page: *20*; Line: *25*; Roll: *CSSCT1901_89*.

[5] 1911 census, 2 April 1911, Census 1911 276/00 002/00 010.

[6] Google Maps, Streetview of Smithfield Farm Monikie, https://www.google.co.uk/maps/place/Carmyllie,+Arbroath,+Angus+DD11/@56.570812,-2.731188,3a,90y,20h,90t/data=!3m4!1e1!3m2!1su5MT1kvMR4W3N_-9K5oUWQ!2e0!4m2!3m1!1s0x48868a59d91c56a7:0xe305ea0c15439d24!6m1!1e1, Accessed 24 August 2014.

[7] Op cit 1901 census.

[8] Op cit 1911 census.

[9] Commonwealth War Graves Commission website, STURROCK, CHARLES GARDYNE, http://www.cwgc.org/find-war-dead/casualty/896599/STURROCK,%20CHARLES%20GARDYNE, Accessed 26 August 2014.

[10] Alyth Guardian, *The War*, 29 November 1918.

[11] Photograph by the Author, taken 19 October 2014.

[12] Wilkie, Irene, *South West Fullerton Farm*, Photograph from personal collection.

[13] Departmental Roll Book Regimental Numbers, Black Watch Museum archive,

[14] Wilkie, Irene, *Charles Sturrock's letters from Nigg Camp, June 1916*, Personal collection.

[15] Op cit Departmental Roll Book Regimental Numbers.

[16] Medal card, *S/15059 Charles Sturrock*, Ancestry.com. British Army WWI Medal Rolls Index Cards, 1914-1920 [database on-line]. Provo, UT, USA: Ancestry.com Operations Inc, 2008.

[17] The National Archives of the UK; Kew, Surrey, England; WWI Service Medal and Award Rolls; Class: WO 329; Piece Number: 1353.

[18] "ronmarsden", Entry onto The Black Watch Forums website, *Black Watch badges from my collection*, Post #450 on 17th May 2013, 18:50, http://blackwatchforums.co.uk/showthread.php?11469-Black-Watch-Badges-from-my-collection/page45, Accessed 23 November 2014.

[19] Kerr, Iain, Rootsweb website contribution, Re: [WW1] WW1 Soldiers Who Died CD/Lookup, Fri, 01 Mar 2002 04:55:29 +0000, http://archiver.rootsweb.ancestry.com/th/read/GREATWAR/2002-02/1014958529, Accessed 29 April 2014.

[20] Baker, Chris, The Long Long Trail website, *The Black Watch (Royal Highlanders)*, ©1995-2014 ~ Chris Baker/Milverton Associates Ltd ~ All Rights Reserved, http://www.1914-1918.net/blackwatch.htm, Accessed 27 October 2014.

[21] Wilkie, Irene, *Charles Sturrock*, Photograph from personal collection.

[22] Wikipedia web site, *Fall of Baghdad (1917) "General Maude's entry into Baghdad, 11 March 1917"*, http://en.wikipedia.org/wiki/Fall_of_Baghdad_%281917%29, Accessed 4 October 2014.

[23] Forces War Records website, *Unit History: Black Watch (Royal Highlanders)*, https://www.forces-war-records.co.uk/units/236/black-watch-%28royal-highlanders%29/, accessed 27 October 2014.

[24] War diaries - Divisional Troops: 2 Battalion Black Watch (Royal Highlanders), WO 95/4713, The National Archives, September/November 1918.

[25] Alyth Guardian, *The War*, 29 November 1918.

[26] Op cit Commonwealth War Graves Commission website, *STURROCK, CHARLES GARDYNE*.

[27] Wilkie, Irene, *Charles Sturrock's Grave*, Photograph from personal collection.

[28] Commonwealth War Graves Commission website, BEIRUT WAR CEMETERY, http://www.cwgc.org/dbImage.ashx?id=2800, Accessed 26 August 2014.

[29] Photograph by the Author, taken 4 May 2014.

[30] Photograph by the Author, taken 6 February 2015.

[31] Photograph by the Author, taken 19 October 2014.

Trooper Alexander Bruce

Alexander Bruce was the eldest child in the large family of Robert Bruce, a coachman from Caithness and Annie Bruce (née Glen) of Brechin, Angus. Alexander was born at Seaton, St Vigeans near Arbroath on 3rd January 1885.[1,2,3] At the time of the 1901 census, the family were living at Cardean by Meigle and Alexander is described as an "ordinary" agricultural labourer.[4] By 1911 his parents, Robert and Annie, were living in The Square in the centre of Meigle where they continued to live throughout the First World War.[5,6]

The Square, Meigle[7]

Prior to the outbreak of the War, Alexander emigrated from Scotland to Canada where he settled in Red Deer in Alberta, working as a motor mechanic.[8]

Red Deer, Alberta[9]

Alexander was in Red Deer at the outbreak of war, and enlisted there on 10th August 1914. His attestation papers from the Valcartier Camp in Quebec show that he had served as a regular soldier in the armed forces prior to his enlistment[10] and, on 13th September, he joined the Royal Canadian Dragoons.

Royal Canadian Dragoons Badge and Flag[11]

Within days, on 25th September 1914, Alexander was among the Dragoons who boarded the troop ship, HMTS (His Majesty's Transport Ship) Laurentic, at Valcartier to begin their journey across the Atlantic.

Some years earlier, in 1910, the Laurentic had gained attention for racing across the Atlantic in pursuit of the SS Montrose, on board which the murderer, Dr Crippen, was trying to evade justice with his lover, Ethel Le Neve. Despite the Montrose having 3 days head start, the Laurentic was the first to arrive in New York and Crippen was duly arrested.[12] Following conversion to an armed merchant cruiser in 1915, she became "HMS Laurentic" but she sank on 25th February 1917 after striking mines laid by the German submarine, U-80, off Malin Head on the north coast of Ireland resulting in the loss of 350 crew and £5 million of gold bullion,[13] of which all but 22 of the 3211 gold bars have since been recovered.[14]

HMTS Laurentic[15]

Returning to the events on 1914, the Laurentic sailed down the St. Lawrence River to the rendezvous point of Gaspé Bay, where she joined a fleet of over 30 transport vessels, together with an escort of warships under HMS Charybdis. This fleet were originally due to sail to Liverpool but the destination was changed to Southampton, before being changed again to Plymouth, due to concerns about the danger from U-boats in the Channel. [16,17]

The Canadian Expeditionary Force at Gaspe'Bay
2 October, 1914.

Gaspé Bay, Quebec, 2ⁿᵈ October 1914[18]

The Laurentic berthed at Plymouth on 17th October and, after a train journey to Amesbury and an 11 mile march, the Dragoons arrived at Pond Farm Camp on Salisbury Plain, where they were to remain for several months.[19] During this time the rain was almost incessant and flooding became a serious problem.[20] Whilst at Pond Farm Camp, Alexander Bruce also suffered the indignity being laid up for a few days from being bitten by one of the horses.[21]

Canadian Cavalry Brigade Waiting for Inspection by King George V,
5ᵗʰ November 1914
(The Royal Canadian Dragoons are in the foreground)[22]

Despite many months of training for a mounted cavalry role, the Royal Canadian Dragoons finally embarked for France on 4th May 1915 to perform a dismounted, infantry role in the trenches of the Western Front.[23]

On 15th June 1915, the Royal Canadian Dragoons were part of the 1st Canadian Division in trenches near the village of Givenchy. Following the disastrous battle of Festubert, the Division were to provide a diversionary attack to support a French offensive further south. Their objectives that day were the German strongholds H2, also known as "Duck's Bill", and H3, a redoubt known as "Stony Mountain". The assault was to be preceded by intense artillery bombardment and the detonation of a mine under the Duck's Bill redoubt. The sappers digging under No Man's Land reached the water table short of their objective and so were unable to proceed any further. They therefore decided to increase the charge to 3000 lbs. of ammonal.

Although the charge blew a huge crater, the German stronghold was relatively undamaged. However, many Canadians were casualties of the blast and the debris buried both soldiers and an important depot of bombs for the assault. The resulting shortage of bombs was compounded by a German shell blowing up another bomb depot. Despite this the Canadians managed to take the forward German trenches but, due to the intensity of the German counter-attack and the shortage of bombs, they were unable to hold their gains and fell back on 16th June.[24]

Alexander must have been very much involved in these actions as, during these events on 16th, he received a blow to his head from a German rifle butt which was to render him unconscious.[25]

Alexander was admitted to a field ambulance for first aid, before being transferred to No.1 Casualty Clearing Station at Choques where his wound was re-dressed. Three days later he was transferred again to No 4 Stationary Hospital at St Omer, before a further transfer to No.4 General Hospital at Versailles on 27th. During this time, Alexander began showing signs of shell shock. He was admitted to No.6 British Stationary Hospital at Le Havre where he was described as being delirious for five days. Initially he took no interest in those around him and would not speak but then Alexander began to show some improvement, though he remained very nervous and excitable and was unable to walk unaided.

He returned to England aboard the hospital ship, Oxfordshire, on 16th July, and was then admitted to the Royal Victoria Hospital at Netley in Southampton before being transferred to the Canadian Convalescent Hospital at Monks Norton near Folkestone.[26]

HMHS Oxfordshire[27]

By the beginning of October, Alexander was well enough to start working in a motor shop at the cavalry depot at Shorncliffe. He was transferred from the Royal Canadian Dragoons to the 1st Canadian Cavalry Brigade Supply Column and, by late January 1916 was deemed well enough to serve once again in France.

Although he had recurring problems in May 1916 and also had to be admitted to hospital for sunstroke in August, he remained in active service until February 1917, when he was admitted to No.3 General Hospital at Le Treport. He then returned to the UK and was treated for neurasthenia (a clinical term that was a historical precursor to the more common term of "shell shock" in the context of WW1)[28] in the No.4 London General Hospital at Denmark Hill (now King's Hospital)[29]

At the beginning of May, Alexander was transferred yet again, this time to Bermondsey Military Hospital, where he remained until September before a further move to the Ontario Military Hospital at Orpington. The decision was then made for his return to Canada. However, this would not be for another six months and after yet another transfer to the No.5 Canadian General Hospital, Kirkdale in Liverpool he finally boarded the hospital ship, HMHS Araguaya, for his final transatlantic journey.[30]

HMHS Araguaya at Newport Docks [31]

Despite further treatment in Calgary and in Edmonton, the army recognised that Alexander would never again be fit for service and he was formally discharged from the forces on 14th July 1918.[32] Two years later, on August 25th 1920, Alexander died of cardiac failure "due to service", in the Colonel Belcher Military Hospital in Calgary, Canada[33] and was buried in Calgary Union Cemetery.[34] Though he died almost a year after the end of the war, Alexander's name appears on the Meigle War Memorial.

Colonel Belcher Military Hospital, Calgary[35]

Alexander Bruce's Grave, Calgary Union Cemetery[36]

Two of his brothers were also to serve in the War. His younger brother, Robert, enlisted on 16th March 1915 and served with the 6th Battalion Black Watch. He appears to have been fighting in northern France, just south of the Ypres salient in early September 1916 when he was wounded and five of his comrades from the same Battalion were killed. Robert's wounds were sufficiently serious for him to be discharged on 23rd May 2017.[37,38] Robert died over 10 years after the end of the war, on 13th August 1929, in Stobhill Hospital, Glasgow from "meningo-myelitis myocarditis".[39] However, the family gravestone in Meigle churchyard attributes his death as "from war effects".[40] Despite this, Robert's name does not appear with Alexander's name on the Meigle War Memorial.

A third brother, John, was reported to have been the first man in Meigle to volunteer. John served with the Army Service Corp, Motor Transport Division and survived the war.[41,42]

The Bruce Family Gravestone in Meigle Churchyard[43]

Alexander, Robert and John had 6 other siblings, though three died in infancy. Tragically, one of their brothers, James, was accidentally washed overboard from the SS Ben Ledi in the Red Sea on 1st January 1930 and was drowned.[44] None of the family appear to have had any offspring of their own and so their line of the Bruce family died out.

SS Ben Ledi[45]

References

[1] Birth Registration, *Alexander Bruce,* (Statutory Births 319/00 0007), 1885 Births in the District of St Vigeans in the County of Forfarshire, p3.

[2] 1891 census, 5 April 1891, *Parish: Liberton; ED: 2;* Page: *3;* Line: *17;* Roll: CSSCT1891_368.

[3] 1901 census, 31 March 1901, Parish: *Meigle; ED: 3;* Page: *3;* Line: *11;* Roll: *CSSCT1901_122.*

[4] Op cit 1901 census.

[5] Op cit Commonwealth War Graves Commission website, BRUCE, ALEXANDER.

[6] 1911 census, 2 April 1911, *02/04/1911 Bruce, Robert [Census 1911 379/00 002/00 002]*

[7] Postcard from Author's collection: *THE SQUARE, MEIGLE,* c.1918.

[8] Service Files of the First World War, 1914-1918 - Canadian Expeditionary Force, *834 Alexander Bruce,* Library and Archives Canada, RG 150, Accession 1992-93/166, Box 1197 – 3.

[9] Horse Industry Conference Red Deer Alberta website, http://ohemesatas.keep.pl/horse-industry-conference-red-deer-alberta.php, Accessed 28 December 2014.

[10] Op cit Service Files of the First World War.

[11] National defence and the Canadian Forces website www.forces.gc.ca, Volume 3, Part 1: Armour, Artillery and Field Engineer Regiments - ARMOUR REGIMENTS, THE ROYAL CANADIAN DRAGOONS, http://www.cmp-cpm.forces.gc.ca/dhh-dhp/his/ol-lo/vol-tom-3/par1/arm-bli/RCD-eng.asp, Accessed 1 September 2014.

[12] Nicoll, Mark M, *The SS Laurentic & the SS Montrose: A story of murder, disguise, and a trans-Atlantic chase.* http://www.titanic-whitestarships.com/The%20Dr.%20Crippen%20Story.htm, Accessed 28 December 2014.

[13] Clarkson Andrew, TITANIC-TITANIC.com website, *SS Laurentic,* http://www.titanic-titanic.com/laurentic_1.shtml, Accessed 28 December 2014.

[14] Irish Underwater Council website, *The Laurentic's golden allure,* http://diving.ie/news/the-laurentics-golden-allure/, Accessed 5 March 2015.

[15] Borge, Solem, Norway Heritage – Hands across the Sea website, *S/S Laurentic (1), White Star Line*, Copyright © Norway Heritage, http://www.norwayheritage.com/p_ship.asp?sh=laur1, Accessed 29 January 2015.

[16] Duguid, Colonel A Fortescue DSO BSc RSA, *Official History of the Canadian Forces in the Great War 1914-1919 General series vol 1*, J O Patenaude, Ottawa, 1938, p89-111.

[17] The Great War Primary Documents Archive website, *1st Canadian Troop Convoy*, http://www.gwpda.org/naval/1cdncvy.htm, Accessed 28 December 2014.

[18] Gathering Our Heroes website, *The Canadian Expeditionary Force at Gaspe Bay 2 October 2014*, © Gathering Our C-K Heroes, http://www.gatheringourheroes.ca/wp-content/gallery/world-war-i/cef-gaspe-bay-2-oct-1914-1-1.jpg, Accessed 28 December 2014.

[19] Op cit, Service record, *Alexander Bruce*.

[20] Op cit Duguid, Colonel A Fortescue DSO BSc RSA, Official History of the Canadian Forces in the Great War 1914-1919, p128-129.

[21] Op cit, Service record, *Alexander Bruce*.

[22] Ben Murray and Benjamin Moore website, The Great War, http://www.2bens.com/page7.htm, Accessed 1 September 2014.

[23] Op cit Duguid, Colonel A Fortescue DSO BSc RSA, Official History of the Canadian Forces in the Great War 1914-1919, p158 and p445.

[24] Op cit Duguid, Colonel A Fortescue DSO BSc RSA, Official History of the Canadian Forces in the Great War 1914-1919, p477-499.

[25] Op cit, Service record, *Alexander Bruce*.

[26] Op cit, Service record, *Alexander Bruce*.

[27] Imperial War Museum, FL 17221 *Hmhs Oxfordshire*, http://media.iwm.org.uk/iwm/mediaLib//19/media-19704/large.jpg, Accessed 29 January 2015. *At a quay*, http://www.roll-of-honour.com/Ships/HMHSOxfordshire.html, Accessed 28 December 2014.

[28] Presley, John PhD, Neurasthenia and the Cure of Literature: Robert Graves, Siegfried Sassoon, Andy Collins. http://www.sergeantbackagain.com/sergeant_back_again_book/neurasthenia.php, Accessed 5 March 2015.

[29] Op cit, Service record, *Alexander Bruce*.

[30] Op cit, Service record, *Alexander Bruce*.

[31] *"Who's Who In Newport"*, The Williams Press Ltd., 1920. accessed via Newport Past Web Site, *HM Hospital Ship Araguaya (RMSP Co.) at Newport Docks*, http://www.newportpast.com/gallery/photos/php/photo_page.php?search=world%20war&search2=yyyyyy&pos=50, Accessed 28 December 2014.

[32] Op cit, Service record, *Alexander Bruce*.

[33] Library and Archives Canada; Ottawa, Ontario, Canada; War Graves Registers: Circumstances of Death; Record Group Number: RG 150, 1992-93/314; Volume Number: 267.

[34] Op cit Commonwealth War Graves Commission website, BRUCE, ALEXANDER.

[35] Wikipedia, *Burns Manor*, http://en.wikipedia.org/wiki/Burns_Manor, Accessed 28 December 2014.

[36] Canadian Virtual War Memorial website, Government of Canada, *In memory of Trooper Alexander Bruce August 25, 1920*, http://www.veterans.gc.ca/eng/remembrance/memorials/canadian-virtual-war-memorial/detail/2765075?Alexander%20Bruce, Accessed 28 December 2014.

[37] Baker, Chris, The Long Long Trail website Great War Forum, *Robert Bruce 6th Black Watch*, http://1914-1918.invisionzone.com/forums/index.php?showtopic=194481, Accessed 1 September 2014 .

[38] Alyth Guardian, MEIGLE MAN WOUNDED, 22 September 1916.

[39] Death registration, 1929 Deaths in the District of Springburn in the County of Lanark, p327.

[40] Bruce family gravestone, Meigle churchyard.

[41] People's Journal (Stirling and Perth Edition) MEIGLE, 15 January 1916.

[42] Alyth Guardian, *MEIGLE MAN HOME*, 16 June 1916.

[43] Photograph by the Author, taken 3 March 2014

[44] Op cit Bruce family gravestone.

[45] Edinburgh's War 1914-1918 website, *Ben Ledi,* © The University of Edinburgh 2014, http://www.edinburghs-war.ed.ac.uk/commerce/ben-line, accessed 28 December 2014.

Map of Locations around Meigle

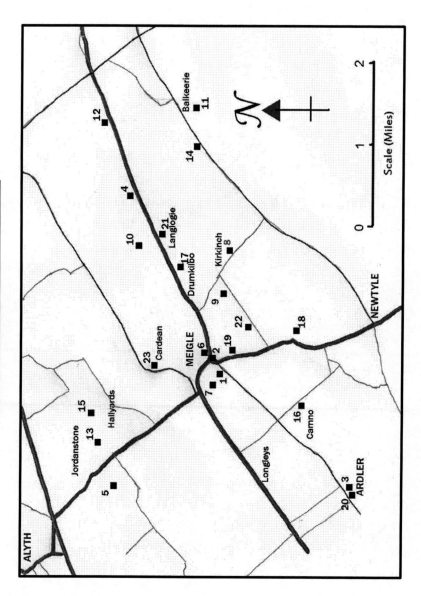

Key to Locations Around Meigle

1. – Meigle War Memorial
2. – Meigle Churchyard
3. – Ardler War Memorial
4. – Arnbog Farm
5. – Balhary House
6. – Bank Cottage, Meigle
7. – Balmacron House (Old Balmacron)
8. – Kirkinch Croft
9. – Myreside Farm
10. – Drumkilbo Tileworks
11. – East Nevay Farm
12. – Castleton of Eassie Farm
13. – West Jordanstone Farm
14. – Kirkton of Nevay
15. – Hill of Hallyards
16. – East Camno Farm
17. – Drumkilbo Cottages
18. – Nether Mill
19. – Melbourne House, Dundee Rd. Meigle
20. – Bentham Street, Ardler
21. – Langlogie
22. – South West Fullerton Farm
23. – Cardean

133